Nourish Your Soul

Swami Mukundananda is a world-renowned spiritual teacher, an international authority on mind management, and a bestselling author who earned his degrees from the prestigious IIT Delhi and IIM Calcutta. He worked with a multinational firm for a short while before renouncing a promising career to enter monkhood. He studied the Vedic scriptures at the feet of Jagadguru Kripaluji Maharaj. For four decades now, he has been sharing his vast knowledge through his books, lectures, and life-transformation lectures.

Every day, Swamiji meets hundreds, and even thousands, of people from all walks of life. His steadfast positivity exudes hope, clarity, and a sense of purpose to those who connect with him. He has deeply affected the lives of millions who have been drawn by his profound integrity, charismatic personality, and passion to serve. Despite his hectic schedule, those who encounter him experience his warmth and compassion and feel deeply touched by his humility. Swamiji's lectures are humorous, his arguments are logical and well-laid out, and most of all, his advice is practical. His lectures on social media platforms are loved and followed by millions. Swamiji divides his time between India and the US.

swamimukundananda.org
facebook.com/Swami.Mukundananda
instagram.com/Swami_Mukundananda
linkedin.com/in/swamimukundananda
twitter.com/Sw_Mukundananda
youtube.com/c/swamimukundananda

Other Books by the Author

7 Divine Laws to Awaken Your Best Self
(Also available in Hindi)

7 Mindsets for Success, Happiness and Fulfilment
(Also available in Hindi, Gujarati, Marathi, Oriya & Telugu)

Bhagavad Gita: The Song of God

Golden Rules for Living Your Best Life

Questions You Always Wanted to Ask

Science of Healthy Diet

Spiritual Dialectics

Spiritual Secrets from Hinduism: Essence of the Vedic Scriptures

The Art & Science of Happiness

The Power of Thoughts

The Science of Mind Management
(Also available in Gujarati & Telugu)

Yoga for the Body, Mind & Soul

Books for Children

Essence of Hinduism

Festivals of India

Healthy Body Healthy Mind: Yoga for Children

Inspiring Stories for Children (set of 4 books)

Mahabharat: The Story of Virtue and Dharma

My Best Friend Krishna

My Wisdom Book: Everyday Shlokas, Mantras, Bhajans and More

Ramayan: The Immortal Story of Duty and Devotion

Saints of India

Nourish Your Soul

Inspirations from and Lives of Great Saints

Swami Mukundananda

RUPA

First published by
Rupa Publications India Pvt. Ltd 2024
7/16 Ansari Road, Daryaganj
New Delhi 110002

Sales Centres
Bengaluru Chennai Hyderabad
Jaipur Kathmandu Kolkata Mumbai Prayagraj

Copyright © Radha Govind Dham, Delhi 2024

The views and opinions expressed in this book are the author's own and the facts are as reported by him which have been verified to the extent possible, and the publishers are not in any way liable for the same.

All rights reserved.

No part of this publication may be reproduced, transmitted, or stored in a retrieval system, in any form or by any means, electronic, mechanical, photocopying, recording or otherwise, without the prior permission of the publisher.

This book is designed to provide information and motivation to our readers. Readers are solely responsible for their choices, actions, and results, and the author and publisher assume no liabilities of any kind with respect to the implementation of principles discussed in this book, including any lifestyle changes.

P-ISBN: 978-93-6156-349-2
E-ISBN: 978-93-6156-282-2

First impression 2024

10 9 8 7 6 5 4 3 2 1

The moral right of the author has been asserted.

Printed in India

This book is sold subject to the condition that it shall not,
by way of trade or otherwise, be lent, resold, hired out,
or otherwise circulated without the publisher's prior consent,
in any form of binding or cover other than that in which it is published.

This book is dedicated to my beloved Spiritual Master, Jagadguru Shree Kripaluji Maharaj, who illuminated this world with the purest rays of divine knowledge and devotion. He taught us by His example, the importance of nurturing souls with love and care, to help them realize a glorious future. He gave us the supreme process of building a noble value system by teaching selfless divine love. I am confident that by His blessings, this book will be helpful in inspiring and elevating seekers, thereby creating a better world for all of us.

Contents

Introduction	1
1 Meerabai	5
2 Adi Shankaracharya	29
3 Soordas	49
4 Tukaram	69
5 Kabirdas	90
6 Ravidas	107
7 Andal	124
8 Ramanujacharya	142
9 Purandara Dasa	166
10 Vallabhacharya	186
11 Tyagaraja	205
Glossary	224
Guide to Hindi Pronunciation	227
Let's Connect	231

Introduction

*I*ndia is known as the land of spirituality. It has been graced by innumerable holy personalities and Saints who left an indelible mark on the spiritual consciousness of humankind. These great luminaries blessed the world by disseminating timeless teachings and illuminating the path to the highest realizations of Divinity.

Lives of these extraordinary souls reveals the sublime art of devotion and the path to spiritual perfection. As instruments of God, they held within them a treasure trove of transcendental wisdom and boundless divine love. They continue to be revered, not only for their oneness with God but also for the inspiration and guidance they left behind.

These Saints achieved the ultimate goal of human life—union with the Divine—and became beacons of light for others on the path of spiritual awakening. They were living embodiments of the eternal Truths of the scriptures. For most, the depth of their wisdom was unfathomable and their magnanimity unimaginable but even more inspiring was their God-intoxicated consciousness. In the heart of every Saint lay unconditional, all-consuming selfless love for the Supreme.

Upon reading about Meerabai, Soordas, Tukaram, Andal, and others, one learns that love is not an abstract notion but an elevated state of constant communion with the Divine. These

Saints exemplified the ideal: God is love, and love is God. As a result, their very presence inspired the awakening of profuse devotion in the hearts of others.

Such enlightened beings are truly very rare. They are palpably distinct, epitomizing the virtues of compassion, humility, serenity, and mercy. Their aura exudes purity and love for all. Transcendentally situated, they are equanimous, dispassionate, and free from pride. They engender a passionate zeal to serve humanity with the attitude of sacrifice and complete surrender to God. With eyes of wisdom, they see the One in all and all in the One.

Undoubtedly, Saints are the embodiment of purity and goodness, being endowed with God's infinite love and grace. Consequently, their mere presence makes a place holy. The Shreemad Bhagavatam states:

tīrthī-kurvanti tīrthāni svāntaḥ-sthena gadābhṛitā

(verse 1.13.10)

'Elevated devotees transform wherever they go into a pilgrimage site, for they hold God in their heart.'

It suffices to say that great Saints in history were divine beings possessing realized knowledge of God and revelling in His bliss. As we study their lives, we find that while the goal remained the Absolute Truth, each Saint had a unique interpretation of Vedic texts and philosophy. They imparted teachings based on time, prevailing circumstances, and the condition of the souls during their era. Adi Shankaracharya revived the teachings of *Advaita Vedanta* while Ramanujacharya presented *Vishishta Advaita*. Vallabhacharya propagated *Shuddha Advaita vada*, and many Saints of the Bhakti Movement focused on personal devotion and experience of God.

Unequivocally, they all broke down barriers of caste, creed, and rituals, propelling souls towards the Supreme based on eternal principles. Each expressed their outpourings of divine sentiments through kirtans, dance, poetry, and literature. Their deeply touching compositions continue to provide spiritual guidance to souls even today.

Clearly, such Saints are our spiritual role models from whom we learn about our purpose in life, virtuous conduct, devotion, and inner transformation. Their biographies reveal that just like us, they too faced personal trials in the form of financial distress, social inequality, and censure. Many experienced less-than-ideal familial conditions and encountered unsurmountable problems. However, unlike us, they remained unperturbed in the face of adversity. They endured hardships perceiving them as an opportunity for spiritual growth. In doing so, they taught lessons in equanimity, faith in the Divine, and positive thinking. The Bhagavad Gita states:

> *mātrā-sparśhās tu kaunteya śhītoṣhṇa-sukha-duḥkha-dāḥ*
> *āgamāpāyino 'nityās tāms-titikṣhasva bhārata*
>
> (verse 2.14)

Shree Krishna explains that fleeting perceptions of happiness and distress arise from contact of the senses with the sense objects. These are ephemeral; they come and go like the seasons. Thus, one must learn to tolerate them without being disturbed.

These Saints veritably lived the principles enunciated in our scriptures and became paragons of philosophical truths. Their messages were universal—offering spiritual illumination and defining meaningful purpose for souls. They taught the perfect synthesis of devotion, wisdom, and action. And invited us to open our hearts to walk the path of Truth and seek the Divine within.

This book is a humble tribute to 11 remarkable God-centered Saints who graced the land of Bharat. While their sacrifices, sublime status, and spiritual wealth cannot be entirely captured in words, it is important to bring forth their teachings as inspiration for generations to come. To truly benefit from the lives of these holy personalities, we must wholeheartedly immerse ourselves into their life stories. As you read about each of them, envision their life unfolding before you. Feel their association and presence by your side. Doing so will bestow benefits as the *Chaitanya Charitamrit* states:

> 'sādhu-sango', 'sādhu-sango' sarv-śhāstre koy
> lav-mātro sādhu-sange sarv-siddhi hoy
>
> (*Madhya Leela*, 22.54)

'The scriptures reveal that by even a moment's association with a true Saint, one can attain spiritual perfection.' Association is not merely physical presence; reading about them and consuming their wisdom is also tantamount to their satsang.

It is my sincere desire that you find your love for God growing exponentially as you savour the biographical accounts and teachings of some of the greatest souls who walked this planet. May their stories become the guiding light of your life and propel you towards spiritual fulfilment and perfection.

1

Meerabai

Meera, better known as Meerabai, was a pre-eminent bhakti saint of the sixteenth century. She was a mystic poet and one of the greatest lovers of Bhagavan Shree Krishna. She revered Him as her Beloved and embodied the purest sentiments of selfless love for her Giridhar Gopal. What she taught by her living example cannot be learnt merely by reading books. Episodes from her life so deeply touched people's hearts that they acquired the nature of legends, passed on from generation to generation.

At a time when women adhered to strict social norms, Meerabai boldly proclaimed her exclusive devotion and fidelity to Shree Krishna. Consequently, her life was fraught with immense opposition and condemnation from both—family and society. Despite this, Meera remained true to her principles and her path.

In time, she transformed from Meera, the princess, to Meera, the ascetic. She is often depicted in pictures wearing a simple ochre sari, with prayer beads on her wrist and tanpura in hand, absorbed in thoughts of Krishna. This portrayal of hers has become iconic for lady monks.

Meera's spiritual fervour is profusely evident in her bhajans.

Through kirtans, she professed her unyielding devotion and adoration for Shree Krishna. At times, she sang about her Divine Beloved's infinite glories. Sometimes she expressed her frenzied state of longing in separation. And other times, she declared her ecstatic love.

Since Meera's bhajans were primarily composed in native Rajasthani and Braj bhashas (languages), they were very accessible to the populace. Meera's poetry stirred people's imagination with the noblest bhakti sentiments of faith and yearning for God. They became inseparable from the Bhakti Movement in North India. Amazingly, they have stood the test of time and continue to be held in the highest regard by devotees and scholars alike.

Meerabai's life is a beautiful treasure chest of inspiration for seekers on the path of *prem* (divine love). It also presents invaluable ideals to emulate for those who aspire to attain the highest level of communion with God.

Birth and Early Childhood

Saint Meerabai was born around the year 1498, in the village of Kudaki, in the Merta district of Rajasthan, to a royal household. Her father, Rao Ratan Singh, was the second son of Rao Duda, the king of Merta. Her great-grandfather, Jodha, established the now-famous city of Jodhpur.

Meera's birth took place on the auspicious day of Sharad Poornima, at noontime, when the sun was in its full glory overhead. For this reason, she was named Mihir, meaning 'Sun'. In due course, her name was changed to Meera. Yet, true to its original meaning, she brightened the world with the radiance of her love!

From childhood itself, Meera's disposition was unmistakably distinct from other children. She was not interested in toys and games. Meera's mother tried hard to get her to play with friends but had no success. It was as if some unknown personality was already attracting her mind and not permitting her to become worldly.

Meera's grandfather, Rao Duda, had immense faith in saints and profound devotion towards them. He would regularly invite sages to his palace, serve them, and listen to their words of wisdom with great attention. Meera would sit for hours in the satsang of these saintly personalities. This further enriched the inherent devotional sanskars she carried from birth. As a result, from her earliest years, her mind was drawn deeply into spirituality.

Events in Meera's life unfolded in an astonishing sequence, revealing how God was forging her for the work that lay ahead of her.

Meera Is Taught Ashtang Yog Sadhana

When she was four, Meera accompanied her grandfather, Rao Duda, on a pilgrimage to the famous temple of Ranchhodrai in Dakor, Gujarat. On their return, she asked, 'Dadaji! The saint who visited us recently had explained that God is everywhere. Then, why did we travel so far to have His darshan? Is God not present in Merta as well?' Rao Duda realized the profound truth in her words.

A short while later, they halted beside a tranquil river where a saint was sitting in deep meditation. Meera was fascinated with the yogi's serenity and sat beside him. On opening his eyes, the yogi was struck by the little girl's ethereal presence. Sensing that she was not an ordinary child, he inquired, 'Who are you, my child?'

The four-year-old Meera responded graciously, 'I am the daughter of Rao Ratan Singh, the son of *param sant sevak* Rao Duda.'

The yogi was impressed by her immaculate phraseology. He took Rao Duda's permission to teach yogic sadhana to Meera and accompanied them back to the palace. The yogi guided Meera through the different steps of Ashtang Yog, culminating in samadhi. After four days, he asked what she perceived in her meditation. Meera responded, 'I see the light of thousands of suns.'

The yogi was astounded. He informed Rao Duda that his teachings were complete. Rao Duda exclaimed, 'In just four days?' The yogi humbly replied, 'It was I who learned from her. Her purity and profound values far surpass my own. What can I teach her? I am fortunate to have been in the presence of such a divine soul.'

Rao Duda looked at Meera and marvelled that such a pious soul had been born in his family. He developed a deep admiration for his granddaughter. On the other hand, Meera's mother became increasingly worried about her devotional inclination. She visualized her daughter as a princess who would one day become a queen and oversee monarchical responsibilities.

Meera's Introduction to Music and Kirtan

Holy men continued to grace Rao Duda's palace. One day, a saint with great musical talent arrived. Seeing him sing with a tanpura, Meera was immediately captivated. She sat with rapt attention and felt her heart swell with bhav (devotional sentiments) as he continued to sing. The saint recognized Meera's devotion. It is said only a heart wounded in love understands its own kind. Likewise, only a devotee truly comprehends another devotee's heart.

On Meera's request, the saint began teaching her to sing. She was a quick learner. One day, the saint requested Meera to sing in front of the family gathering. As she began, it was not mere verses, but the outpourings of her soul overcome with divine love that burst forth. On witnessing the spiritual qualities of his granddaughter, Rao Duda was mesmerized. He heartily encouraged Meera to continue her devotion through songs. Thereafter, music was integrated into Meera's life, complementing the sadhana she had learnt from the yogi. However, her spiritual quest still lacked the supreme direction.

This was when one more saint arrived from Vrindavan, the holy land of Shree Krishna. He solidified Meera's spiritual calling towards Shyamsundar. He filled her head with the Glories and Pastimes of the Master of the gopis. Let us relish her bhav through one of her bhajans:

> baso more nainan meṅ nandalāl
> mohanī mūrati sāñvarī sūrati naiṇā bane visāl
> adhar sudhāras muralī rājat ura baijantī māl
> chhudra ghaṇṭikā kaṭi taṭ śhobhit nūpur śhabd rasāl
> mīrā prabhu santan sukhadāyī bhagat vachhal gopāl

'May Nandalala always grace my eyes. May the captivating Form and beautiful face of Shyam never leave my sight. His lips pour forth pure nectar as He plays the flute, and a *vaijantimala* graces His chest. Tiny bells decorate His waist, and the sound of His ankle bells is wonderfully sweet. The Master of Meera is Gopal, who is particularly loving towards His devotees and brings immense joy to the saints.'

Meera now had a path she could follow—the path of love for Shree Krishna. She would spend her time engrossed in bhakti by meditating on Vrindavan and singing for her Lord's pleasure.

Turning Point—Receiving Giridhar Gopal

Meera's life took a glorious turn upon the arrival of another saint. He possessed a beautiful deity of Shree Krishna, whom he called Giridhar Gopal. Meera would be in awe of the deity as she watched the saint worship Him daily. In her heart of hearts, she longed for a similar deity to serve and worship.

The saint would closely observe Meera and quickly recognized her entrenched devotional sentiments. In one of the satsangs, he requested Meera to sing a bhajan. She was delighted and expressed her innermost longing and pangs of separation from her Shyamsundar. Let us savour her bhav through one of her most famous bhajans, paying special attention to the intensity of her bhav:

> *he rī maiṅ to prem divānī mero darad na jāṇai koy*
> *darad kī mārī ban ban doluṅ baid milyo nahī koy*
> *nā maiṅ jānū āratī vandan, na pūjā kī rīt*
> *liye rī maine do naino ke dīpak liye sanjoye*
> *ghāyal ki gati ghāyal jāṇai, jo koī ghāyal hoy*

jauharī kī gati jauharī jāṇai kā jin jauhar hoy
mīrā kī prabhu pīr miṭegī jad baidh sāñvariyā hoy

'O Dear, I am madly in love, but no one understands my pain. Tormented by pain, I wander here and there, but I find no healer. I do not know the rituals of worship or the ways of prayer. My eyes alone serve as the two lamps for worship. The condition of the wounded is only understood by another who is wounded. The struggle of a jeweller is only understood by another jeweller acquainted with knowledge of jewels. So, Meera keeps wandering, finding no healer for her pain. Meera's pain will only be relieved when the healer is the Dark One, Shree Krishna, Himself.'

The saint could not believe his ears. He had never heard anyone express such profound love for the Lord. He understood the 'jewel' Meera was in search of was Shree Krishna, the Crest Jewel of Rasik Saints. The saint continued staying at the palace for another two weeks, but then it was time for him to depart. Meera was tormented by the thought that the saint would leave soon and dreaded the void his departure would create in her heart. She wondered if she could ask him for the deity but hesitated. Why would anyone give away their beloved *Iṣhṭa Dev*?

Sometimes God works in mysterious ways. The sadhu felt deeply blessed to have encountered such a special soul and wished to reciprocate by giving Meera a gift. That night, the deity appeared in his dream and directed him to give the idol of Giridhar Gopal to Meera before leaving. The next morning, the sage called Meera and asked if she would like to serve his Giridhar Gopal. Meera enthusiastically agreed as her long-cherished dream was coming true. Upon seeing Meera's expression, the saint could not stop smiling to himself. He entrusted the deity to Meera and left.

Meera's life now revolved around her Giridhar Gopal. She formed an eternal bond of sacred love and adoration with Him, so much so that every action became an act of worship. She would sing to her Darling and talk to Him for hours. She danced in divine ecstasy to please Him. Every day, she would bathe and adorn her Giridhar with the finest clothes and jewels. If she sensed that her Beloved's smile had faded, she would worry—perhaps He did not like the food, or maybe He was thirsty, or possibly there was something else that was troubling Him. She would weep for hours until she saw Him smiling again. Meera's life and heart were drenched in blissful Krishna bhakti that knew no bounds. As her love intensified, she lost herself in the service of her Lord.

Meera Meets Her Guru

Meera was now basking in the love of her Giridhar Gopal. However, she had one unfulfilled desire—to find a Guru. For her devotion to fructify, she coveted the guidance and grace of a realized saint. This was when news came of the arrival of Kashi's great saint, Sant Ravidas. Meera was elated to know this. She had finally found her Spiritual Master.

Meera left the pooja of her Beloved Shree Krishna, ran to meet Ravidas, and started serving him. Was this justified? The *Hari Bhakti Vilas* states it definitely was.

ye me bhakta-janāḥ pārtha na me bhaktāśh cha te janāḥ
mad-bhaktānām cha ye bhaktās te me bhakta-tamā matāḥ

(verse 10.133)

Shree Krishna tells Arjun: 'Those who consider themselves to be My direct devotees are not truly My real devotees. However, those who are devoted to My devotees are indeed My true devotees.' Giridhar Gopal was dearest to Meera's heart, but Gurudev was even dearer.

Sant Ravidas recognized Meera's life purpose right away. He placed an *ektara* (string instrument) in her hand and said, '*Beti* (daughter), your spiritual path is that of bhajan.' With this innocuous gesture, he gently nudged Meera towards the work that lay ahead of her.

From that day on, Meera took the ektara and made bhajans her life. Though she used to sing earlier too, with Sant Ravidas' blessings, her sadhana now reached unparalleled heights. With the *ektara*, Meera sang songs for her Giridhar Gopal. As her devotion intensified, day by day, her personality turned graver. She lost all sense of hunger, grew sleepless, and became utterly disinterested in the world. Her consciousness became entirely absorbed in her Beloved.

Meera Gets Married

Meera was now in her youth. Grandfather Rao Duda had grown old and was bedridden. It was evident his time was limited. This greatly worried Meera, for in the family, he alone understood her pining heart. Whenever a marriage proposal would come, he would support her decision to decline it. But what would happen after he was gone?

As anticipated, Rao Duda soon passed away, and the topic of Meera's marriage began to dominate all household conversations. The family received a proposal for liaison with Kunvar Bhojraj, son of Rana Sangha, the famous king of Chittorgarh. Meera's mother was insistent that this time she would not accept 'No' for an answer.

However, Meera astounded her mother by announcing that she was already married. 'I am a Rajasthani with Rajput blood in me,' she said. 'Married Rajput ladies never look at another man, even in their dreams, but now you want me to marry this Bhojraj?'

Mother was stunned and asked, 'You are already married! Whom are you married to?'

Meera reminded her when, many years ago, a marriage procession was passing by. Seeing the bridegroom, she had asked who her groom would be. Mother had responded that the deity in her hand, Giridhar Gopal, was her husband. 'Since then, my mind accepted Shyamsundar as my Beloved,' Meera declared. 'He alone is the Master of my heart.'

Let us savour Meera's mystical outpourings through this bhajan:

> *mere to giridhar gopāl, dūsaro nā koī*
> *jāke sir mor mukuṭ mero pati soī*
> *koī kahe kāro, koī kahe goro, liyo hai aṅkhiyāñ khol*
> *koī kahe halako, koī kahe bhāro, liyo hai tarājū taul*
> *asuvan jal sīnch sīnch, prem bel boī*
> *ab to bel phail gayī, ānand phal hoī*
> *tāt māt bhrāt bandhū, āpaṇo na koī*
> *chhāḍ gayī kul kī kān, kā karīhai koī*

'Giridhar Gopal is the only One who is mine. He alone is my Husband, who wears the peacock feather on His crown. Some say He has a dark complexion, others claim He is fair, but I have seen Him with open eyes. Some say He is light, others assert He is heavy, but I have measured Him on the scale of my heart. I have cried torrents of tears and nurtured the sapling of love. The plant is now flourishing and bestowing the fruit of joy. Father, mother, brother, and friends—none of these are mine. I have transgressed the dignity of my dynasty, and I do not care what anyone says or does.'

Meera's mother was not swayed by her reasoning. She found it irrational for her daughter to claim a deity as a husband. Societal norms were very different five centuries ago. Girls, especially, did not have the option to defy parents in matters of marriage. Meera's wedding was thus finalized, and she resigned to her fate, 'O Gopal! If this is Your will, then so be it.'

The wedding proceeded, but Meera arrived at the *mandap* (wedding setup where the bride and groom walk around the fire for their vows) with her deity of Giridhar Gopal in hand. She held Him even while circumambulating the sacred fire with Bhojraj. In her mind, she was consecrating the marriage to her real husband, Shree Krishna. While people look in the world for their soulmate, Meera knew no other than Shyamsundar.

The truth is that God is our eternal and sole Companion. All our worldly relationships will cease upon death. In our past lives, we had different sets of relatives whom we do not remember now. Similarly, our current relatives will also be separated from us one day—when either they or we depart to the afterlife. This is why the scriptures explain that worldly relatives do not qualify as soulmates.

Our real soulmate is the one who stays eternally with our soul.

The word for 'a relative' in Sanskrit is *sambandhi*. It refers to that personality with whom we have a 'complete and eternal relationship.' Such a relative is God. He is seated in our hearts and accompanies us from lifetime to lifetime. As His little fragments, our every relationship is with Him. The Bhagavad Gita states:

gatir bhartā prabhuḥ sākṣhī nivāsaḥ śharaṇam suhṛit
prabhavaḥ pralayaḥ sthānam nidhānam bījam avyayam

(verse 9.18)

Shree Krishna says: 'I am the Supreme Goal of all living beings, and I am also their Sustainer, Master, Witness, Abode, Shelter, and Friend. I am the Origin, End, and Resting Place of creation; I am the Repository and Eternal Seed.' Hence, from the transcendental perspective, God alone is our Soulmate.

Meerabai Rebels to Assert Her Single-Minded Devotion

Meera now travelled with Bhojraj from Merta to Chittorgarh. As she entered the palace, her mother-in-law took her to the temple of their family deity, Baan Mata. She instructed Meera to pay obeisance before their dynasty's *Iṣhṭa Devi*. Meera refused, boldly declaring, 'My body, mind, and soul are dedicated solely to the lotus feet of Giridhar Gopal. Meera will not bow before any other god.'

Such defiance! This stubbornness angered her mother-in-law and sowed the seeds for a lifetime of hostilities for Meera. Why did she refuse to offer obeisance to Baan Mata, who was a form of Mother Durga? Would her exclusive love for Shree Krishna be tarnished? This could not be the compelling reason in her mind because a Krishna bhakta sees God in all and can bow before anyone. More likely, she was emphasizing her uncompromising single-minded devotion to her Giridhar Gopal.

Married life had gotten off to a shaky start. However, Meera was a dutiful wife to Bhojraj. Yet, her love was solely reserved for Giridhar Gopal, whom she adored with all her heart and soul. Fortunately for her, Bhojraj, too, had a noble side to him. He empathized with his wife's saintly nature and did not object to her decision to maintain her chastity.

Meera's daily routine included finishing her household chores and then withdrawing to her pooja room. There, she would sit with Giridhar Gopal, dance ecstatically, and sing heartfelt songs. She would be immersed in divine reveries, contemplating loving pastimes with Shree Krishna. This was her only passion and joy.

In a few months, the *Gangaur Vrat* (a day of fasting) came. It was a fast that Rajasthani women observed with great reverence. Unmarried women worshipped goddess Parvati to get a suitable husband. Married women kept it for the long life of their husbands. Meera's sister-in-law, Udabai, advised her to adorn the best ornaments and observe the *Gangaur Vrat* for Bhojraj.

Meera refused, insisting that her husband, Giridhar Gopal, was absolutely hale and hearty. Udabai sternly admonished her for this silliness. She commanded Meera to do the *solaha shringar* (sixteen adornments) like all other women. Again, Meera countered, saying external decorations were futile. Inner virtues, such as tolerance, faith, and humility, were more important.

Meera's disobedience aroused the wrath of Udabai. She had already antagonized her mother-in-law. Now, her sister-in-law was also disgruntled with her.

Conspiracies that Ultimately Transformed the Hearts of Adversaries

Udabai started to plot with maids in the palace to discredit the new bride. They instigated Bhojraj by telling him they had witnessed Meera talking to her paramour on many nights. Such behaviour was a matter of shame for the royal family of Chittor. Hearing this, Bhojraj's anger knew no bounds. He hurried to Meera's quarters—with a sword in his hands—to kill her secret lover.

On his way, someone stopped the prince and cautioned him to verify whether the news was indeed a fact. Bhojraj, though upset and visibly shaken, composed himself. He stood outside Meera's room and listened intently from behind the doors. He heard Meera joyfully singing.

syām mane chākar rākho jī
girdharīlāl chākar rākho jī
chākar rahasūṅ bāg lagāsūṅ nit uṭh darasaṇ pāsūṅ
vṛindāvan kī kunj galin me terī līlā gāsūṅ
chākarī me darsaṇ pāūṅ sumiraṇ pāūṅ kharachī
bhav bhagati jāgīrī pāūṅ tīnū bātāṅ sarasī
mor mukuṭ pitāmbar sohe gal baijantī mālā
vṛindāvan me dhenu charāve mohan muralīvālā
mīrā ke prabhu gahir gambhīrā sadā raho ji dhīrā
ādhī rāt prabhu darsan dīnhe prem nadī ke tīrā

'O Shyam, keep me as Thy servant. As Your vassal, I will plant

Your garden. Every morning, Your sight will be my reward. In the arboreal lanes of Vrindavan, I will sing Your praises. Thy sight and remembrance will be my wages, and my day will pass in Your devotion. Wearing a beautiful peacock crown, a yellow waist cloth, and a glittering gem necklace, Mohan, the flute player, is grazing cows in Vrindavan. Meera's Lord is always patient and solemn. In the middle of the night, on the banks of the river of love, I request Your sight. O Shyam, keep me as Thy servant.'

Meera was fully absorbed in confessing her love to Giridhar Gopal. Bhojraj broke open the door and rushed in with his sword drawn. 'Who is your lover?' he demanded. 'I will finish him off!'

Meera remained completely unperturbed. She remarked, 'Whose life will you take? I was talking to my Soul-Beloved. Will you use the sword on Him?'

Bhojraj was perplexed and asked, 'Who is your soul beloved?'

'Giridhar Gopal,' Meera answered. 'I was conversing with Him.'

Bhojraj was profoundly moved by the purity of Meera's response. He accepted his wife as an extraordinary saint who had unparalleled love for God. Upon seeing this, even Udabai's heart softened, with remorse for her grave misunderstanding. They had never encountered a devotee like Meera before. Bhojraj's respect and admiration deepened, and her position in the household became even more favourable.

One day, Bhojraj told Meera to ask for a gift. She responded that she deeply missed the satsang environment of her parents' home. If a temple were to be built within the palace premises, she could then invite saints and host satsangs.

Bhojraj responded affirmatively. He said that rarely in life does one get an opportunity to do such pious deeds. Having received it, he would not miss the chance. He constructed a temple for Meera inside the palace compound so that she could easily continue her devotion.

Giridhar Gopal's Infallible Love and Protection for Meera

The newly constructed temple in the royal palace soon became a hub for satsang. Meera was in her element in the midst of sadhus and devotees. She would sing self-composed bhajans and dance with unfettered zeal. She reveled in serving saints without caring for the palace grapevine or the local gossip.

The family grew anxious seeing holy men frequent the palace daily and interact with Meera. This was not apt for the princess of Chittorgarh. However, Meera remained undeterred by family censure. She continued to sing and dance with divine joy. One day, news of the blissful satsangs reached Emperor Akbar. He was a powerful Mohammedan ruler of Delhi. He revered saints of all denominations and wished to see the famed female saint, Meera, whose bhajans he had heard.

There is an apocryphal tale about Akbar's encounter with Meera. It states that Akbar disguised himself and took Tansen, his chief musician, with him to Chittorgarh. He entered the temple incognito and participated in the satsang. Akbar was enchanted by Meera's rapturous love for God. He sensed her divinity as she sang and danced. At the height of her emotions, in devotional trance, Meera fell unconscious. When she regained awareness, Akbar introduced himself as the Badshah of Delhi. He insisted on offering her gifts out of respect and admiration. However, Meera graciously declined, so finally, Akbar placed a pearl necklace before Giridhar Gopal and left.

The news of the royal daughter-in-law of Chittorgarh receiving a gift from Badshah Akbar reached Rana Sangha, and then Bhojraj. Rana Sangha's Rajput pride was hurt. He made it known that Meera had disgraced their family and needed to atone for it. The matter was so emotionally charged that Bhojraj was obliged to support his father. Meera asked if sacrificing her life would suffice, to which Rana Sangha agreed.

Meera embraced her Beloved Giridhar Gopal and left the palace with thoughts of finally uniting with her Lord. She reached the river where she intended to drown herself. She dazzled brightly with divine love in her heart and Govind's name on her lips. Standing on the banks, Meera surrendered her being and prepared to jump. Just as she leapt into the flowing waters, someone seemed to hoist her out. It was the Lord of her heart, Giridhar Gopal, who had come to protect her. Seeing Him, Meera fell unconscious.

She woke up in the arms of her Beloved Gopal. He smiled and said, 'Your life with your mortal husband and relatives is over. You are now forever Mine.' Shree Krishna explained that He had finished her external world, and now there was only one path for her—the path of divine love.

Shortly thereafter, Meera received word that her father-in-law,

Rana Sangha, and husband, Bhojraj, had been killed in fighting. Meera was now a widow and free to pursue her path.

Meera Fearlessly Faces Challenges with Unshakeable Faith

Bhojraj's cousin, Rana Vikramjeet, now reigned the kingdom of Chittorgarh. Vikramjeet disliked Meerabai and was irked by her ways. He even considered her promiscuous. Meera did not discard her jewellery after her husband's death. When people questioned her behaviour, she responded, 'My Husband, Giridhar Gopal, is fine and can never die!' Her defiance only fueled Vikramjeet's vexation further. Meera made her struggles with Rana Vikramjeet the subject of many of her bhajans.

Rana finally planned to get rid of Meera. He knew every morning she would walk across the palace courtyard to the temple with a flower garland for Shree Krishna. One day, Vikramjeet left a lion loose in the courtyard. Udabai understood Rana's intentions and forewarned Meera of the danger. However, Meera remained unaffected. She responded by saying, 'If Rana gets annoyed, he will throw me out of the palace. But where will I go if my Giridhar Gopal gets angry?'

Meera proceeded to the temple unafraid. Rana was watching through his window as Meera walked with garland in hand. To his utmost surprise, the lion became as docile as a house cat, and she visited the temple unscathed.

In another incident, Vikramjeet sent a crate with a snake inside, saying it was a gift from Giridhar Gopal. Meera opened it, but instead of the snake, found an image of her Lord.

Rana was furious and consulted the *vaidya* (doctor) for a deadly poison. Five gold bowls were filled with poison and sent to Meera with the message that they were the *charanamrit* of Shyamsundar (nectar after bathing the feet of the deity) that had arrived especially from Vrindavan.

Once again, Udabai warned Meera of Rana's evil intentions: 'Beware of his treacherous plan to poison you.' Meera remained undaunted and declared, 'If it is the *charanamrit* of my Lord, I have nothing to fear.' She drank the poison and remained unharmed.

As Rana's atrocities intensified, Meera realized it was futile to continue living in Chittorgarh. She left the palace and proceeded to Vrindavan, the sacred land of her Beloved Shree Krishna. She resided near Nidhivan and subsisted on alms while engaging in devotion with even more fervour.

Encounter with Jiva Goswami

While Meerabai was in Vrindavan, she heard of Jiva Goswami, a prominent disciple of Chaitanya Mahaprabhu. Eager for his darshan, she went to his ashram and requested his audience. Jiva Goswami's disciples conveyed her request to their Guru. He said, 'Tell her that I am a sanyasi and do not meet any women.'

The disciples carried their Guru's message to Meera. She replied, 'I had heard that there is only one purush (man) in Vrindavan—Brajraj Kumar Shree Krishna. Who is this other man who says I do not give darshan to women?'

God is the Supreme Purush, while all of creation is His prakriti (nature). This includes material nature and the individual souls. So, when the disciples conveyed Meera's statement to Jiva Goswami, he came running barefoot to meet her. He understood she was situated on a sublime transcendental realization, far higher than his own.

While living in Vrindavan, Meera composed many bhajans. One of the more popular ones is shared below for you to savour:

> ālī rī mohe lāge vṛindāvan nīko
> ghar ghar tulasī, ṭhākur sevā, darśhan govind jī ko
> nirmal nīr bahat yamunā ko, bhojan dūdh dahī ko
> kunjan kunjan phirat rādhikā, śhabd sunat muralī ko
> mīrā ke prabhu giridhar nāgar, bhajan binā nar phīko

'O friend! I adore Vrindavan, where in every home, Tulsi is revered, and the deity of Govindji is worshipped. The pure waters of the Yamuna flow, and milk and yoghurt are the staple foods. O friend! I love Vrindavan dearly. There, the deity sits on a jewelled throne adorned with Tulsi in His crown. O friend! I cherish Vrindavan immensely. In Vrindavan, Radhika wanders from grove to grove, drawn by the sound of His flute. O friend! I hold Vrindavan in the highest regard. Giridhari, the Master of Meera, teaches that without devotion, life is dull. O friend! Vrindavan is my heart's delight.'

Meera Leaves a Legacy of the Highest Expression of Love

After a couple of years, Meera travelled to Dwarika. This was the place where almost 5000 years ago, Shree Krishna had established His capital city. In Dwarika, Meerabai stayed for eight years at the historic temple of Dwarikadhish.

In the meantime, after her departure from Chittorgarh, the kingdom experienced a series of disasters—drought, extreme cold, and so on. Learned advisors explained to Rana Vikramjeet that these catastrophes were the karmic reactions for insulting a great devotee. Feeling remorse, Rana sent a delegation to reconcile with Meera and bring her back to Chittor.

It was noon when Rana's representatives arrived at the temple and respectfully begged her to return. Meera heard their message but then looked at the deity of Dwarikadhish. With tears in her eyes, she cried out to her Beloved, 'Leaving You, O Giridhari, where should I go now?'

Soon, a light enveloped Meera, and she looked astonishingly glorious. She walked directly into the temple's inner sanctum and merged into the deity of Shree Krishna. All that was left behind was her *chunari* (veil). She had left the world *sasharir* (with her body). In memory of her devotion, even today, Dwarikadhish is adorned with Meera's *chunari*.

Through her hymns and conduct, Meerabai taught pure and selfless love for God. Such *para bhakti* exists in the spiritual realm. Occasionally, great devotees descend from God's divine Abode. They teach us about divine love and how to attain it. Meerabai was one such soul. She practised *madhurya bhav*—loving the Lord with conjugal sentiments. *Madhurya bhav* is considered the sweetest sentiment of devotion because it allows for the most intimate connection with God. Such bhakti is characterized by intense and spontaneous love that is untinged by selfishness. No barriers remain between the lover and Beloved. There is complete oneness between them, as God forgets His godliness and becomes enslaved by the devotee.

Meerabai's bhakti was completely steeped in the sentiment 'Giridhar Gopal alone is my All-in-All.' She renounced her worldly relationships without a second thought. Her journey and destination were one—her Soulmate, Shree Krishna. She longed for her Beloved in separation, sighed and sobbed for Him, and perpetually lived in divine anguish.

This intense yearning for God is the pinnacle of bhakti. It is known as *viraha*. When love ripens, it is natural for the senses and mind to hanker for the Divine. At this stage, the devotee ardently desires to have darshan of the Lord, to offer love and service. Yet, God stays hidden because He needs the devotee to purify the remaining vestiges of impurities. This longing keeps the devotee's heart in agony. It is a profound pain akin to the feeling of a fish out of water or the breathlessness of someone on the brink of drowning.

The experience of pain in the heart while yearning for God is called *viraha vedanā*. It is supremely purifying. Just as gold sparkles even more when placed in the fire, the inferno of separation burns all vices and worldly attachments, making the heart a fit receptacle for divine love. Hence, *viraha* is all-auspicious as it leads to spiritual union with the Divine.

The gopis of Vrindavan illustrated this as their love grew stronger and more selfless in the absence of Shree Krishna. His thoughts pervaded their very being. Wherever they looked, they perceived their Beloved—in their homes, in the fields, in the forest groves, in their works, and so forth. Ultimately, every movement of their consciousness became worship for His pleasure.

Similarly, in her divine longing, Meerabai demonstrated an

unparalleled level of love. As her heart pined, she discovered her Beloved's presence in everything and everyone. In this way, Meerabai left behind teachings of love expressed in its most exalted form. Undoubtedly, anyone who practises such sublime bhakti will reach the reservoir of eternal joy and love, Shree Krishna.

2
Adi Shankaracharya

In the rich spiritual lineage of Bharat, Adi Shankaracharya has been one of the most influential Vedic philosophers and Acharyas. He is considered by many as the saviour of the Sanatan Dharma in his times. In addition to writing many sacred works and commentaries, he also established 10 sanyas sampradayas that continue even today. Appreciating the importance of his life and works requires an insight into the socio-religious situation prevailing at that time.

After Shree Krishna closed His pastimes on the earth, Kali yug began. With the passage of time, religious practices were degraded. People were committing animal sacrifices in the name of yajnas. They were misinterpreting the holy books and had become mired in rituals. This was when the Buddha appeared and preached his gospel of compassion and purity of thought. He taught Dharma and Sangha but not devotion to God.

In due course, however, the vigour and purity of the Buddha's teachings were forgotten. His followers made huge viharas and began worshipping the Buddha as God. They evolved specious logic to defend their ideologies. To add to the confusion, Buddhist tantrism grew in popularity, with its many *yanas*, such as *Vajra-yana, Sahaj-yana, Guhya Samaja-yana*, and *Kalachakra-yana*.

Since Buddhism had become the state religion, followers of Vedic dharma were reduced to a minority. Those who remained were divided into fanatic and quarrelling sects. Adherents of *Saṅkhya, Nyāya*, and *Vaiśheṣhika* propounded their dry logic, while ignoring the practice. Followers of *Mimansa* restricted themselves to *karm kaṇḍ*, believing the celestial abodes as the highest attainment. Other denominations, such as the *Kapalikas, Pancharatras, Ganapatyas, Pashupatas, Kalamukhas, Tantrikas*, and *Kaulas* asserted bizarre and even atheistic views. Their internecine quarrels disillusioned people from the lofty ideals of Hinduism.

Spiritual wisdom was thus conspicuous by its absence. Needless to state, Hinduism had reached its lowest ebb, and there was an urgent need for its revival before it collapsed into oblivion. It was at this time that Adi Shankaracharya appeared.

His teachings of non-dualism charmed the Buddhist philosophers back into the fold of Hinduism. With masterful commentaries on the Vedic scriptures, not only did he reconstruct faith in people's hearts and reestablish the glorious position of the eternal Vedas but also united society around common values and principles. Thus, the great Acharya course-corrected the journey of countless souls.

Blessing of Bhagavan Shiv

Estimates about when Shankaracharya was born vary widely. While records of the Govardhan Matha at Puri state his birth as

2500 years ago, historians believe he came in the eighth century ce. Many hagiographies exist describing Shankaracharya's life. The most popular is the *Madhaviya Shankara Vijayam*.

It is believed that Shankara appeared on the Shukla Panchami of the month of Vaisakha in the Hindu calendar. His parents, Shivaguru and Aryamba, were devout brahmins. They resided in the village of Kalady in Kerala, on the banks of the Periyar River. The couple prayed to their *Iṣhṭa Dev*, Bhagavan Shiv, for a child. When he was born, they named him after the Lord, as Shankara, meaning 'one who ushers peace and goodness'.

Shivaguru was a great Vedic scholar and began tutoring his child in Sanskrit and the *Kavyas*. Consequently, at the young age of four, Shankara became proficient in the Puranas and poetic construction. As he grew, his brilliance and spiritual powers started manifesting. One such episode is mentioned here.

After his sacred thread ceremony, as was the tradition, the five-year-old Shankara visited people's homes to collect alms. A penurious old lady offered Shankara the only edible thing at her home—a dried amla (gooseberry). The word 'amla' also refers to the circular disk-like structure atop temples. While the lady placed the amla in Shankara's bowl, she blessed him, saying: *karatala-amalakavat* 'May your self-knowledge shine in the palm of your hand, like the amla atop the temple.'

Young Shankara was so moved by the poor woman's generosity that he recited the 21 verse *Kanakadhara Stotra* in praise of goddess Lakshmi, which resulted in a shower of *amalakas* (amlas made of gold) in her courtyard. Some people believe the lady was Mother Saraswati (goddess of learning and wisdom), who had come in disguise to bestow benediction on the divine child.

The Call of God Beckons Shankara

When Shankara was still five, his father passed away. He was then sent to study at a gurukul. There, Shankara's extraordinary intelligence and poetic talent impressed everyone. He mastered many Vedic scriptures, and his fame spread far and wide. This attracted the attention of kings across South India. Many invited the erudite boy to their court with the promise of rewards. But Shankara was committed to his higher purpose, and no amount of wealth or opulence could divert his focus.

Shankara's young mind was intent on the pursuit of a monastic life, much against the wishes of his widowed mother. She could not think of letting go of her only child. But when the call of God arises, it is the strongest desire in life. Who had the ability to stop him?

A divine leela unfolded to facilitate Shankara's getaway from home. Astrologers had predicted that he would live only until he was eight. One day, when he had gone to bathe in the river, a crocodile grabbed his leg. Hearing her son's pleas for help, Aryamba came running but was powerless to help. As she cried profusely, Shankara addressed her, 'Mother, I have only a few moments left. Please permit me to take sanyas and fulfil my dream.'

Aryamba instantly agreed to her son's wish. Miraculously, at that very moment, the crocodile released Shankara's leg, and he emerged unscathed from the waters. Aryamba thanked God for saving her son and realized she could not bind him with motherly affection. She blessed him for his spiritual journey ahead. Before departing, Shankara promised his mother he would be beside her during her last breath.

Years later, when Shankara received word about his mother's imminent death, he fulfilled his promise. With his mystic abilities, he travelled by the skyward path to meet her. On her deathbed, Shankara instructed his mother to practise devotion to Shree Krishna. He also fulfilled his obligation by lighting her funeral pyre, even though it was a forbidden ritual in monkhood.

Meeting His Guru

The quest for a Guru made young Shankara walk 2000 kilometres from South Kerala to the banks of Narmada River in Central India. There, he met Govinda Bhagavadpada, also known as Govindacharya. The self-realized sage formally initiated Shankara into the order of Vedic sanyas. Under his tutelage, Shankara studied and mastered all the Vedic scriptures in a short span of time.

Shankara's love for his Guru is revealed in a famous episode. Once, during the rainy season, the Narmada River was in spate. Govindacharya was sitting in dhyan in a cave by the riverbank. Disciples rushed to warn him of the rising waters. But the young Shankara, who dutifully served his Guru every day, did not want him to be disturbed. He placed his *kamandal* (water pot) at the entrance of the cave, and it gathered all the gushing water. Later, when the flood subsided and Govindacharya emerged from the cave, he commended Shankara's sharanagati (surrender). Gurudev blessed him to gain eternal glory by writing commentaries on holy books.

The Guru also instructed Shankara to travel across the length and breadth of ancient Bharat to spread the true message of the Vedas and revive Sanatan Dharma. Shankaracharya then proceeded to Kashi—the historical seat of scholarly learning.

The Teacher of Advaita

In Varanasi, also popularly known as Kashi, the Acharya began accepting disciples and training them to be instruments in his work. Among them was Sananda, who later became known as Padmapada. Two other well-known students were Trotakacharya and Hastamalak.

Spirituality is often perceived as a pursuit to be practised on a mountainside. However, Shankaracharya was determined to bring it to the villages, towns, and cities of Bharat. In his *digvijayi yatra* (victory journey) across the nation, he tirelessly strived to infuse Vedic wisdom into the hearts of all. With utmost compassion, he raised the consciousness of all who cared to hear him.

People spend their entire life chasing money, palatial houses, power, and fame. However, in his famous *Prashnavali*, Shankaracharya questions the nature of success:

jagad jitam kena? 'Who shall conquer the world?'

He then provides his deeply spiritual answer:

mano hi yena 'One who conquers the mind.'

So much to gain from so few words of Shankaracharya! We all wish to upgrade our lives, but we do not realize that our mind contributes the most to our life's experiences. It creates our perceptions of happiness and distress. If it goes astray, it robs our inner joy, dragging us into a cesspool of miserable thoughts and feelings. But if effectively trained, the mind becomes our biggest resource for optimism, contentment, determination, and joyfulness. The wonder is that 2000 years ago, Shankaracharya emphasized the science of mind management as the most useful skill in life.

Shankaracharya condensed the entire *Advaita* philosophy in his *Brahma Jnanavali Mala* with the statement: *brahma satyam jaganmithyā jīvo brahmaiva nāparaḥ* It means God is the Absolute Reality; the world of maya is an illusion; the individual soul is non-different from God.

To validate it, Shankara quoted: *aham brahmāsmi*, the famous *mahavakya* from the *Brihadaranyak Upanishad*. It means 'I am one with the Almighty'.

The Vaishnav acharyas who followed Shankaracharya explained that the mantra does not mean the soul itself is God. Rather, as one's hand is one with the body, and as the leaves are one with the tree, similarly, the soul is also one with God.

In fact, Shankaracharya also states the same in his *Vishnu Shatpadi Stotram*:

satyapi bhedāpagame nātha tavāham na māmakīnastvam sāmudro hi taraṅgaḥ kvachana samudro na tāraṅgaḥ

(verse 3)

'O Lord! It is true that You and I are one; and yet, there is a difference. Just as waves arise from the ocean, not the other way around, likewise, we have emanated from You, not You from us.'

Masterful Writings of Knowledge and Devotion

At Kashi, the Acharya began writing books. These became a legacy for the future. Their impact was compounded by his mastery over Sanskrit and powerful writing style. By the age of 16, he had finished writing his major treatises. His wealth of knowledge was reflected starting from his first commentary on *Vishnu Sahasranam* to his later expositions on Bhagavad Gita, the 11 Upanishads, and the *Brahma Sutras*. These latter three together came to be known as *Prasthān Trayī* (three gateways of knowledge).

His other important works expounding on the fundamentals of *Advaita Vedanta* philosophy include the *Vivek Chudamani, Atma Bodha, Aparoksha Anubhuti, Atma-Anatma Vivek, Drig-Drishya Vivek, Vaakya Vritti, Sanat Sujatiya,* and *Upadesh Sahasri*.

Shankaracharya's *Jagannathashtakam, Pandurangashtakam,* and *Krishnashtakam* are some of the best poems in Indian literature. They describe the beauty of Shree Krishna and His various Forms. These compositions convey that unless a soul remembers Krishna, it will continue to rotate in the cycle of birth and death. His popular lines often sung during the famous Jagannath Rath Yatra are:

jagannāthaḥ swāmī nayana patha gāmī bhavatu me

'O Lord of the universe, when will You become visible to my eyes?'

His compositions are famous even today in the arena of Carnatic music and find beautiful expressions in traditional dance forms, such as Odissi, Kuchipudi, and Bharatnatyam. In this way,

Shankaracharya truly inspired souls for millennia on the path of spirituality.

The Acharya also composed innumerable meditative hymns, such as *Saundarya Lahari, Shivananda Lahari, Nirvana Shatakam*, and more. All of these are matchless in sweetness, melody, and thought.

Shankara Debates with Scholars

In those times, throughout India, there was a fragmented understanding of Vedic injunctions. This resulted in people being misled to believe that enjoyment of sensual pleasures was the aim of life. To reform such deficient knowledge, Shankaracharya challenged eminent scholars and various religious leaders through vigorous debates. By winning them through arguments, he made them understand the distilled essence of the Vedas. In this way, Shankaracharya rebuilt the withering pillars of Hinduism.

One such famous debate took place with Mandan Mishra, a well-known *Mimansa* philosopher. *Mimansa* focuses on performing Vedic rituals in pursuit of heavenly pleasures. Shankaracharya wanted to dispel this inferior understanding and reveal higher vistas of Vedic knowledge.

A long-drawn philosophical discussion ensued between Mandan Mishra and Shankaracharya on the relative merits of the *Mimansa* and the *Advaita* viewpoints. The dialogue was of such eloquence, scholarship, and perspicacity that even the celestial gods assembled and attended it for several days. The stakes were high: if Shankaracharya were defeated, he would marry and become a householder. On the other hand, if Mandan was beaten, he would don the robes of a sanyasi.

Mandan Mishra's wife, Ubhaya Bharati, a scholar in her own right, presided over the debate. When she saw her husband unable to withstand Shankaracharya's arguments, she contested that Shankara's victory would be incomplete unless he also defeated her since they were a couple.

The contest then continued between Ubhaya Bharati and Shankara. She questioned Shankaracharya on marriage and relationships, challenging his claim of complete Vedic wisdom. The towering scholar confessed his lack of knowledge in this area since he was a strict celibate and had no experience of family life. He requested some time to study this topic before resuming the debate, which was granted.

Shankaracharya went to a cave along with his disciples. He instructed them to guard his gross body while he left in the subtle body. Then, through his yogic powers, he entered the body of King Amaruka, who had recently passed away and was about to be cremated.

Suddenly, the king, who had been taken to be dead, sat up. His retinue of servants took him back to the palace. There, King Amaruka's wives welcomed him back. They noticed a transformation in their husband's nature but could not understand the reason for it. Shankaracharya then experienced life as a householder.

After a month, with this newfound knowledge, Shankaracharya returned to his physical body, which was being guarded by his disciples. He resumed the debate with Ubhaya Bharati and defeated her. Both Ubhaya Bharati and Mandan Mishra bowed their heads in humility before the wise Shankaracharya. Thereafter, Mandan Mishra became one of his chief disciples and came to be known as Sureshvaracharya.

It was through such brilliant debates that Shankaracharya cleared many contradictions and disseminated true spiritual wisdom. He also travelled with his disciples to the Badrikashram where he climbed the snow-capped mountain in North Badrinath to meet the great Sage Ved Vyas.

Ved Vyas, a *chiranjīvi*, had been living on the earth since Satya yug. Shankaracharya sat with him in a secluded spot. The two learned and saintly personalities deliberated on scriptural principles and their conclusions for seven days. When Ved Vyas realized he could not defeat Shankaracharya, he extended the discussion by another seven days. Finally, impressed by Shankaracharya's prowess, the great Sage blessed him with success in his mission.

Bhagavan Shiv Gives Darshan to Shankara

When Saints descend on the planet, they spread their teachings not just by giving discourses but also by performing many pastimes. These pastimes create immemorable impressions on people's minds and get passed on as lessons for many generations. One such incident occurred when Shankaracharya was on his way to the Ganga for his mid-day ablutions.

A person from a socially marginalized community came directly on his path. Shankaracharya felt his purity could get tainted by being in close proximity to someone from such a background.

He commanded the poor man to clear off the road. The man, however, smiled. He questioned the Acharya as to who was he asking to move from the path—the body or the soul?

If it was his soul, then as per non-dualism, the soul is one with God. Does a difference exist between the reflection of the sun in the Ganga versus its reflection in a lake? Is there any distinction between the space within a golden jar versus the space within a clay pot? Besides, the soul, being one with Brahman, was all-pervading. Then where was the question of it moving?

If the Acharya was referring to the body, it was made up of the elements of the world. These were *mithya* (unreal) in any case, as per Shankara's assertion. So how could anyone's body contaminate another?

The force of logic and conviction in the man's words rendered Shankara speechless. It was an important learning in rising above bodily distinctions. This was the practical application of the *Advaita* philosophy to everyday living. Shankara responded with a hymn called the *Manisha Panchakam*, where *Manisha* means 'wisdom' and *Panchakam* refers to the 'five' philosophical verses. In these verses, he also revered the penurious person as his Guru for shedding the light of wisdom on his ignorance. It is believed that the destitute later revealed Himself as Bhagavan Shiv.

In this way, God and Guru together purge the maladaptive beliefs from our mind. Even today, Shankaracharya's precepts are needed to eliminate discrimination that has pervaded human society beyond caste and creed. The sovereign recipe for this is spiritual wisdom that enables us to see all as the divine soul.

ātmavat sarva bhūteṣhu yaḥ paśhyati sa paṇḍitaḥ
'Those who can see others as the self are the real pandits and true scholars.'

Mother Durga Reveals Herself to Shankaracharya

In his commentary on the Vedant, Shankaracharya had declared that God is *nirgun* (without the gunas), *nirvishesh* (without attributes), *nirakar* (formless), and *akarta* (non-doer). However, after he returned from Badrinath to Kashi, his teachings were assayed in a remarkable incident.

One day, Shankaracharya and his disciples were headed to the Manikarnika Ghat on the Ganga for a bath. His path was blocked by a woman with the dead body of her husband in her lap.

Shankaracharya requested, 'Mother, please give way.'

But the woman continued to cry profusely at the loss of her loved one. Shankaracharya continued to repeat his request while the woman wailed louder.

Finally, the Acharya got irritated and scolded the lady. 'What is the use of crying?' he said. 'Your husband has gone and will not come back.'

Suddenly, the lady turned towards him. 'Why are you asking me?' she blurted. 'Why do you not ask my husband to get up and give way?'

Shankaracharya explained, 'Dear lady, how can your husband's body get up? It is dead and has no shakti.'

The woman again retorted, 'Acharya, in your *Sharirak Bhashya*, you have stated that God does not have any shakti. But we all know that He is the Creator of this world. Can God create this world without shakti? To make such an amazing world, He must possess innumerable powers. And you are saying, He is *shakti rahit* (without energy)? If you are right, then to prove your point, let this dead body without shakti rise and walk off.'

Shankaracharya was stunned into silence. He wondered who this woman was. She had so easily meted him a spiritual defeat. He blinked his eyes, and lo behold! When he opened them, he beheld the sight of Mother Durga, the Adi Shakti, sitting on a lion.

Shankaracharya realized that the Divine Mother had intervened to enhance his realization of the Truth. As he paid his obeisances to Her, he sang praises which came to be known as the *Ananda Lahiri*. In this composition, he admitted that God creates the world with His various shaktis. The Yogmaya Shakti, in the form of Mother Durga, governs the process of *shrishti* (creation), *sthiti* (sustenance), and *pralaya* (dissolution) that takes place through the material energy.

Shankaracharya glorified the formless God in his commentaries but undertook many pilgrimages to worship the myriad forms of the Divine. In this way, he proclaimed the dual nature of God. He composed innumerable verses in praise of Shree Krishna, Shree Ram, Bhagavan Shiv, and Mother Durga.

The Great Unifier of Society

Shankaracharya appeared in an era when innumerable sects followed their own narrow philosophies and quarrelled over the superiority of their individual views and systems of worship. To unite them on common principles, Shankaracharya established the *Pancha Dev Upasana*. In it five principal deities are worshipped—Vishnu, Ganesh, Shiv, Durga, and Surya. This practice is followed in many Hindu homes even today.

Shankaracharya also formulated the system of rituals and rites to be followed in temples which was widely adopted by priests. Establishment of standardized practices in temples was a big step towards the religious and cultural integration of Bharat. In this way, a vast nation, disarrayed with different opinions, was united along common threads.

Shankaracharya had immense organizational abilities too. With great foresight, he established his *mathas* at four different corners of Bharat for championing and propagating the principles of Vedic dharma. These are the Sringeri Matha in Karnataka, Kalika Matha in Dwaraka, Gujarat, Jyotir Matha in Uttarakhand, and Govardhan Matha in Puri, Odisha. He also inaugurated the famous Kumbh Mela, a religious tradition that continues even in modern times, as the largest congregation of pilgrims across the world.

Another significant contribution of Shankaracharya to Sanatan Dharma was the restructuring of the order of sanyas. Under this, the *Dasanami* sanyas tradition was established. Ten *sampradayas* for monks in the *Advaita* tradition were identified and associated with different *mathas*.

With Shankaracharya began the tradition of *Jagadguru*, which means 'Spiritual Master of the world'. After him, the time-honoured title of original *Jagadguru* has been bestowed on four more saints to date: Jagadguru Nimbarkacharya, who established *Dvaita Advaita vada*, Jagadguru Ramanujacharya, who established *Vishishta Advaita vada*, Jagadguru Madhvacharya, who established *Dvaita vada*, and Jagadguru Kripaluji Maharaj, who was conferred the title in 1957 by the Kashi Vidvat Parishat.

A Lesson for His Disciples

During one of his travels, the Acharya reached a village where residents offered him liquor. He accepted their hospitality. His disciples merrily followed him and got drunk. This made him want to teach a lesson to his disciples. So, when he moved to the next village, he drank molten iron in a foundry shop and asked his disciples to emulate him, as they had done earlier. The disciples were ashamed and admitted it was beyond their capacity.

The Acharya went on to explain that descended Saints strive to uplift fallen souls by various means. Not all their works can be comprehended by one's intellect. Therefore, the works of Saints should not be imitated. Rather, the teachings they deliver should be followed. Consider the following example:

A teacher once instructed his students, 'Great personalities should be your role models. You must follow their path.'

One student took the teachings literally. Next day, he arrived early and sat on his teacher's desk. When the teacher entered, the student said to him, 'Go and sit on that empty chair for students.'

The teacher was shocked at what he heard but decided to play along. He sat amongst the class but raised his hand and asked the student, 'Sir, I have a question.'

The student now panicked. How could he answer his teacher's question? He admitted his folly in imitating the instructor.

The teacher then explained, 'When I said we must copy great personalities, I meant you should follow the path they took to become great. Likewise, if you wish to reach where I am today, you will first have to study day and night and become a teacher. Then you can do what I am doing today.'

We mortal souls should not imitate either God or God-realized Saints. We should simply follow the teachings They bestow on us.

His Final Work

Once when Shankaracharya was walking along the streets of Kashi, his attention was caught by an elderly man trying hard to learn Sanskrit grammar from the *Panini Sutras*. Seeing a soul mechanically involved in rote learning pained Shankara's heart. At his advanced age, the man should have dedicated his remaining time to worshipping God.

Death approaches without any forewarning and verses of grammar cannot emancipate one at that final moment. With this strong message, Shankara indited his famous song, *Bhaja Govindam*:

> bhaja govindam bhaja govindam
> govindam bhaja mūḍha mate
> samprāpte sannihite kāle
> nahi nahi rakshati ḍukṛiñkaraṇe

The stotra is a wake-up call to a soul in slumber. The Acharya urges the soul to turn towards God and sing His glories rather than wasting time in non-productive pursuits. The *Bhaja Govindam* is striking in its exotic poetic beauty and perfection of composition.

In his *Prashanavali* also, Shankaracharya affirms developing love for God:

kim karma kṛitvā nahi śhochanīyam?

'What is that work which does not lead to repentance later?'

kāmāri kansāri samarchanākhyam

'One who engages in devotion to Shree Krishna, the slayer of Kansa, has no regrets later.'

In further questions, Shankaracharya also advises aspirants to be situated at the feet of a merciful Spiritual Master. They can then close their eyes without worry and easily cross the ocean of material existence.

People are often puzzled over Shankaracharya's personal inclination towards bhakti, while his fundamental teachings are immersed in *Advaita*. The answer is that the great acharyas teach according to *deśha* (time), *kāla* (place), and *pātra* (circumstance). Shankaracharya was, in fact, an expansion of Bhagavan Shiv. He descended to revive people's faith in the sacred Vedic scriptures. But he came at a time when voidist Buddhist ideas were dominating society. He could not teach bhakti upfront, but at heart, he was always a devotee.

Return to Bhagavan Shiv

When Shankaracharya was 32, he proceeded to Kedarnath along with his disciples. At this holy Abode of Lord Shiv, the

Acharya expressed his desire to give up his material body. He then presented the essence of all his teachings in 10 verses, known as *Dashashloki*. It is said that as the verses were being chanted, Shankaracharya entered mahasamadhi and his body disappeared without a trace. The great Adi Shankaracharya returned to Bhagavan Shiv—the source of his incarnation.

The entire land of Bharat, in fact, all humankind, will remain indebted to Shankaracharya for his works and teachings, which made such a difference in people's life.

3

Soordas

Soordas was an exceptional blind poet-saint of the Bhakti Movement of medieval India. He became popular for his lyrical compositions, imbued with exquisite devotional sentiments for Shree Krishna. Even though he could not see, he was often blessed with divine vision that enabled him to witness Shree Radha Krishna and Their loving Pastimes within his heart. His intense devotion was reflected in his heart-melting bhajans.

Soordas composed songs mainly in the languages of Braj, Hindi, and Avadhi. His writings vividly narrate the sweet, loving pastimes of Lord Krishna as a playful Child, Lover, and Savior. These immensely bolstered the devotional literature on Shree Krishna and the path of bhakti.

Soordas was one of the eight poet-disciples of Vallabhacharya, the founder of Pushti Marg. They were known as *aṣhṭachāp sakhās*, among whom Soordas was regarded as the most distinguished protégé. Vallabhacharya referred to him as an 'Ocean of Devotion'. His penetrating love for Shree Krishna also endeared the Mughal Emperor, Akbar, who was in awe of Soordas' melodious voice and talent.

Even today, seekers and scholars continue to be inspired by

the Saint's devotional intensity and artistic expression. His compositions in praise of Shree Radha Krishna are performed and enjoyed in devotional congregations worldwide.

Birth and Early Childhood

Historians estimate Sant Soordas was born in 1478 CE. Soordas Jayanti is celebrated on the fifth day of the Hindu month of Vaisakha. He was born to a brahmin family in a village called Sihi, near Delhi. His father, Ramdas Saraswat, a scholarly pundit, was very poor. His mother was Jamunadas.

Since his blindness added to the hardships of the financially strapped family, they considered Soordas an inauspicious and unfortunate child. As a result, he was neglected and unloved by his parents. However, their behaviour did not disturb Soordas, instead, it deepened his connection with the Divine.

Ramdas was an expert in music, and although he disliked Soordas, he imparted his knowledge to the young boy. Soordas quickly absorbed all he was taught. Despite being visually impaired, he compensated for it through mental clarity and immersed himself in the study of sacred texts. He also began composing verses that set the foundation for his future as a revered poet-saint.

Renouncing the Family with Faith in God's Protection

Soordas was gifted with the faculty of recognizing omens and the ability to recover lost items. This was displayed in one of his pastimes which eventually liberated him from family life and pushed him on the spiritual journey.

Once, when Soordas' family was going through a particularly hard time, his father was given two gold coins for performing a ritual as a priest. This offered some respite from the family's penury. Unfortunately, the coins were stolen by rats that night. The next morning when Soordas' parents were unable to find the coins, they were heartbroken and could not stop crying over their lost fortune. Soordas was moved to compassion and gently began comforting them with wise words.

'Father, it is not right to lament over worldly possessions,' he said. 'Gold or anything else is just dust. Seek real wealth—the wealth of true love (*prem dhan*).' His father, already distressed by the loss, perceived Soordas' words as more salt in the wound.

The family blamed Soordas for their ill luck with the coins and began beating him. Soordas asked them to stop and promised to reveal the location of the coins. However, he posed a condition that he be allowed to leave the house once the coins were found.

The family agreed since they were desperate to recover the gold. Despite his blindness, Soordas took them to the place where the rats had left the coins. The parents were astonished and realized the divinity of their son. Their hearts filled with love and affection, and they insisted Soordas stay back. However, he warned them, saying, 'The coins will disappear again if you stop me.' Reluctantly, his parents let him depart from home.

Soordas left the house with firm faith in God's shelter. He thought, 'The One who takes care of all beings will also take care of me.'

Saints unequivocally demonstrate steadfast faith in God's loving protection. While we find solace in our insurance policies, bank balances, and worldly relationships as shields from hardships, Saints depend solely on the Lord's grace and take His refuge. Sage Narad expresses this condition of exclusivity:

anyāśhrayāṇām tyāgo 'nanyatā

(*Narad Bhakti Darshan*, sutra 10)

'Reject all other shelters, putting your faith exclusively in God alone.'

How do Saints easily place their trust in the Supreme? They realize God's benevolence and protection towards all, especially the surrendered souls. The Shreemad Bhagavatam states:

pīta-prāye 'mṛite devairbhagavān loka-bhāvanaḥ (8.9.27)

'The Supreme Divine Personality is the Best Friend and Well-wisher of the three worlds.' Even a worldly father cares and provides for his children. God, our eternal Father, does the same on a cosmic scale. Why, then, should we doubt His ability to care for us? He sustains every living being in creation. Think of the trillions of ants on Earth—each one finds food regularly. Have you ever noticed thousands of ants starving in your garden? Nature ensures for their provisions.

Similarly, elephants consume vast amounts of food daily, yet the Universe accommodates their needs too. Just as it provides for the smallest of creatures, it also meets the needs of the largest. This benevolence of Nature is a testament to the unwavering care of our Divine Father.

Exhibiting such faith in the Lord's infallible protection, Soordas left home fearlessly in the quest for spiritual fulfilment. He settled in a village few kilometres away, taking refuge under a tree. Moved by compassion, the villagers regularly brought him food for sustenance. One day, a man named Gopal was searching for his missing cows, when he came across Soordas. The pious man inquired if Soordas had seen his cows. Soordas directed him to a nearby cowshed.

Gopal discovered his cows exactly where he was guided. He was overwhelmed with gratitude and offered one of the cows to Soordas, who humbly declined the offer. However, Gopal insisted on providing him basic lodging and daily food provisions, which he respectfully accepted.

Now Soordas devoted himself to writing and singing bhajans. His melodious voice and soulful compositions drew the local villagers, and the crowds grew with time. Life in the village was pleasant, and 12 years passed by without disturbance.

One day, Soordas reflected on his journey and realized he had been siderailed by the fame received and lost sight of his supreme goal. Resolutely, he left the village and moved to the holy city of Mathura in Braj, settling in a village called Gau Ghat.

There, too, his bhajans attracted a crowd. People would come to listen to his heart-warming renditions and bring food offerings in his service. This continued for another 12 years.

Soordas' Quest for a Guru

Soordas' thirst for deeper spiritual fulfilment continued to guide his path. As he progressed spiritually, he realized he needed a Guru to guide him towards the ultimate goal of God-realization.

Why do Saints emphasize the need for a Guru? The Vedic

scriptures inform us that all souls in the material realm are suffering from an affliction. That disease is not physical, but spiritual. Its name is ajnana, or nescience.

We often attempt to dispel ignorance by educating ourselves, earning degrees, and acquiring qualifications. From the spiritual perspective, however, the ignorance lingers. Despite our academic achievements, we continue to harbour anger, greed, jealousy, pride, and other negativities. So, how do we eradicate the spiritual darkness that has veiled us since countless lifetimes? The Shreemad Bhagavatam states:

anādy-avidyā-yuktasya puruṣhasyātma-vedanam
svato na sambhavād anyas-tattva-jño jñāna-do bhavet
(verse 11.22.10)

In this verse, Lord Krishna explains to Uddhav that since endless lifetimes, the intellect of the soul has been covered by nescience. This cannot go away by self-effort alone; it requires receiving knowledge from a Guru, who is a knower of the Absolute Truth. The syllable *gu* means 'darkness', and *ru* means 'to dispel it'. Hence, the one who dispels our darkness and brings us into the light of knowledge is the Guru.

Satsang with a genuine saint naturally detaches us from the world and develops our attachment to God, giving rise to bhakti in the heart of the disciple. The *Narad Bhakti Darshan* states:

mukhyatastu mahatkṛipayaiva bhagavatkṛipāleśhād vā
(sutra 38)

'Bhakti is attained primarily by the grace of the Guru and marginally by the grace of God.' Hence, one of God's most magnanimous graces is when He brings the soul in contact with a true guru. Through humble and sincere service, one can appease the Guru. Spiritual knowledge and devotion are revealed in the heart of the disciple when the Guru is pleased.

Shree Krishna soon fulfiled Soordas' pure intention of finding a Guru. Mahaprabhu Vallabhacharya, a great devotee of Radha Krishna, decided to stay at Gau Ghat on his way to Braj. Seizing the opportunity, Soordas went to meet the Acharya. He realized he would not be able to see the great Sage, but to him, what truly mattered was that Vallabhacharya would see him. Darshan was, after all, a small matter compared to the Guru's grace.

Sant Soordas reached the congregation and was immediately spotted by Vallabhacharya, who called him closer and asked him to sing a bhajan. He recited a self-composed bhajan, expressing his inner humility.

> *syām, garībani hūñ ke gāyak*
> *dīnānāth hamāre ṭhākur, sāñche prīti-nibāhak*
> *kahā vidur kī jāti-pāñti kul, prem-prati ke lāhak*
> *kahā pāndav kai ghar ṭhakurāī, arjun ke rath-vāhak*
> *kāhya sudāmā kai dhan hau tau, satya prīti ke bāhak*
> *sūrdās saṭh tātaiṅ harī bhaji, āsa ke duḥkh-dāhak*

'In this bhajan, Soordas prays to God with humbleness: "O Dīnanath! You are the Refuge of the destitute, the Savior of the fallen, and a true Lover. Vidur was not of high caste or rich to be showered with love. O Lord! You went to the Pandavas' home under the influence of love and devotion and became Arjun's charioteer. Despite Sudama's poverty, You maintained loyal friendship with him. Soordas says that we should always remember God because He is the only one who can remove the sorrow of surrendered living beings."'

Vallabhacharya was impressed and asked him to continue singing other compositions. Soordas again sang a kirtan of *dainya bhav* (sentiment of humility), expressing his insignificance in front of the Supreme. The Acharya was delighted at his modesty but requested to hear something about the glories of the Lord. Soordas humbly replied, 'Gurudev, I do not know any Leelas of God. How can I sing Them?'

Vallabhacharya understood and directed him to come back after taking a bath in the Yamuna. Soordas obeyed his Guru's instructions. Upon his return, Vallabhacharya instructed Soordas to place his hand on the table of contents page of the Shreemad Bhagavatam and slowly move it down. Vivid images began to form in Soordas' mind as his Guru read the list of divine leelas. The different Pastimes, such as Shree Krishna tending the cows in the forest, Shyamsunder playing with the gopis, and Nandalala in the lap of Yashoda—all played like a movie in Soordas' heart. His heart overflowed with devotion as he witnessed Lord Krishna in all His glory!

Subsequently, the Saint composed numerous poems relating the Leelas from the Bhagavatam, as the Puran was indelibly etched in his mind.

Going to Shrinathji Temple in Braj

Vallabhacharya now decided to continue his journey from Gau Ghat to Braj and took Soordas with him to the temple of Shrinathji in Govardhan.

The Acharya desired to give Soordas the service of singing bhajans for Shrinathji, and so he prayed to the Lord to grace his protégé. Vallabhacharya then inquired from Soordas, 'Were you able to get darshan of Thakurji? What did you see?' Soordas had indeed been blessed with a divine vision of the Deity. As his heart overflowed with reverence and love, he started singing:

> charaṇ kamal bando hari rāī
> jāki kṛipā pangu lāṅgheṅ, andhe ko sab kuch darasāī
> bahiro sunai mūk puni bole, rañk chale chhatra dharāī
> sūrdās swāmī karuṇāmay bār-bār bandau tehi pāī

'I pray to the lotus feet of Shree Hari, whose grace enables the lame to cross mountains and the blind to see. By His mercy, the deaf can hear, the dumb can speak, and the beggar can walk under a royal umbrella. Soordas says, "O merciful Lord, I honour You by bowing down my head repeatedly."'

Vallabhacharya was overjoyed to have found such an eligible candidate for Thakurji's service. He explained to Soordas that his duty was to please the Lord by chanting for Him. Soordas happily carried out this seva, composing and rendering the devotional *padas* (hymns) in Braj language to Shrinathji.

Krishna Serves Water to His Devotee

Vallabhacharya arranged for Soordas to live in a village called Parasauli, near Govardhan, while he continued travelling all over India. Soordas' daily routine involved visiting the temple and singing bhajans to please Thakurji. A young boy named Gopal was assigned to assist the Saint with his needs.

One day, as Soordas was eating, a piece of food got lodged in his throat. The Saint called out for Gopal to bring him a glass of water, but the boy had already left. In his place, the ever-loving real Gopal, Shrinathji, appeared, handing Soordas water in a gold glass.

The next day, there was an uproar in the temple over Shrinathji's missing gold glass. The priests suspected theft either by devotees or robbers. They searched everywhere and finally reached Soordas, where they found the glass in his room. When asked about the glass, Soordas realized that Shrinathji Himself had brought him water. Soordas was overwhelmed by the Lord's magnanimity, and the episode deepened his devotion even further.

Radha Krishna Give Darshan

Soordas often visited people's homes to conduct satsangs. One day, after finishing such a satsang, Soordas was walking back to his home, using his stick to navigate the path.

While walking, he came dangerously close to a pit; two more steps, and he would have fallen in it. However, Thakurji is always watchful over His devotees and had a special eye on Soordas. He manifested and grabbed His devotee's walking stick, chiding, 'Oh Babaji, how careless of you! There is a pit ahead, and you are about to fall. Are you not worried at all?'

Soordas was grateful and said, 'My son, thank you very much. You saved my life.' The childlike Krishna replied, 'Let Me take you to your hut, Babaji.' Shree Krishna held the front of the stick while Soordas held the back-end as they walked along. After a short conversation, Soordas suspected that the Lord had come Himself, as only His voice could be so attractive.

He decided to catch Krishna by slowly extending his hand on

the stick. Shyamsundar realized Soordas' intent and thought, 'This baba is clever. I gave him one finger, but he wants the whole hand.'

Laughing, Krishna mischievously let go of the stick and ran away. He then stated profoundly, 'It is not so easy to catch Me. Great yogis and sages practise meditation and still do not get My darshan in their samadhi. How will you catch Me like this?'

Unfazed, Soordas recited a famous *doha*:

> *hāth chhuḍāye jāt ho, nibal jānike mohi*
> *hirday te jab jāhuge marda badaungo tohi*

'O Shree Krishna, You may slip from my feeble grasp, considering me weak. But if You are truly heroic, try escaping from my heart, where I have seated You forever. Only then will I consider You a real man.'

Soordas challenged the all-powerful God by boldly declaring, 'You cannot leave my heart because I love You, and You are bound by that love.' Such is the power of selfless devotion.

While we commonly use the word 'love' to describe our feelings in worldly relationships, true love is a far more profound emotion. Understand the difference between love, lust, and business.

Lust is driven by the desire for self-pleasure. The dominant thought is 'take, take, take'. Such lust is as far from love as darkness is from light. Now consider the nature of business. It involves a give-and-take mindset: 'I did this for you, now you must do this for me. Otherwise, I do not care about you.'

In contrast to both these, love is a deep and noble affection for others' happiness without seeking personal gain. It is unconditional and selfless. The characteristic of true love is that it remains steadfast even when the beloved behaves poorly. This is because it is selfless; it does not demand reciprocation and willingly overlooks the other's flaws.

The same principle applies to *nishkām bhakti*, or selfless devotion. Even when God behaves adversely, a true lover remains ever happy, perceiving it as His grace. Just as gold is refined by fire, burning away its impurities, likewise, God uses negative behaviour to enhance the purity of the devotee's love and make it more selfless. A poet states:

> *japhā meṅ bhī andāze vaphā hotā hai*
> *dil ka āīnā esase aur safā hotā hai*

'Even disloyalty of the Supreme Lover, God, is His loyalty. The undesirable behaviour becomes a means of grace as it cleanses the heart, removing all self-seeking.'

Though God distanced Himself, Soordas remained unaffected because his love was not tied to Shree Krishna's behaviour or the need for reciprocation.

Later, the divine couple Radha Krishna revealed Themselves to the Saint. They restored his vision and gave darshan. On beholding his Lords with his physical eyes for the first time, tears of joy streamed down Soordas' face.

A few minutes later, Shree Krishna asked, 'What boon can I offer to you?'

Soordas responded, 'Hey Govind! Please make me blind again.'

Astonished, Krishna asked, 'We just gave you vision, and now you want to be blind?'

Soordas explained, 'Maharaj, I have been blind since birth. The first thing I saw was Your divine darshan. Now I do not wish to see anything else, so may this Divine image reside forever in my eyes.'

Accepting his wish, Shree Krishna made Soordas blind again.

Test of Divine Vision

Despite being visually impaired, Soordas could perfectly envision Radha and Krishna with his mind's eyes. His seva at the temple was to sing for Their pleasure. In his bhajan, invariably, there would be a couple of lines describing the *shringhar* (adornments) of the Deity. He perfectly portrayed the expressions, clothing, jewellery, and beauty of Shrinathji.

Vallabhacharya's sons and a local pandit would serve the Deity every day. They would bathe and adorn it, cook food and offer it as bhog, do the aarti, put the deity to sleep at night, etc.

However, Vallabhacharya's sons were sceptical of Soordas' ability to describe the Deity with such accuracy. They thought Soordas had a secret pact with the priests, who might be informing him of the daily attire. So, they decided to test him and kept Thakurji bare that day. Then they eagerly awaited Soordas' reaction.

Soon the curtain lifted to reveal the Deity adorned only with a pearl necklace but bereft of clothing. Soordas smiled serenely as he envisioned the adorable scene. The congregation held their breath in curiosity about what he would sing. Soordas sang the following with great love:

deke rī hari nangam nangā
jalsut bhūṣhan ang birājat,
   basan hīn chhabi uṭhat tarangā
ang ang prati amit mādhurī,
   nirakhi lajit rati koṭi anangā
kilakat dadhisut mukh le mana bhari,
   sūr hañsat braj juvatin sangā

'O Sakhi, look! Today, Shree Krishna stands unclothed. Adorned only with strings of pearls, waves of beauty radiate from His bare form. Every limb exudes unparalleled sweetness; even the Sun and countless cupids are put to shame by His magnificence. Soordas says that the Lord has an enchanting smile and drops of milk on His face as He laughs with the gopis.'

Everyone was amazed and understood that Soordas was blessed with divine vision that allowed him to perceive God in all His splendour.

Soordas could see God clearly in his heart. The question then arises: Why do we not have any perception of His presence like the Sage?

The answer takes us into philosophy—God is divine, while our instruments of perception are material.

We possess three channels to receive information—senses, mind, and intellect. These mediums enable us to gather data and learn about people and things. However, they are made from maya, the material energy, and have a limited purview. Our eyes can only see physical things, ears hear only material sounds, skin can only feel tangible objects, and so forth. On the other hand, the Supreme Divine Personality, who is non-material, is beyond the purview of these instruments of knowledge.

Now the question arises: 'How did innumerable Saints perceive and realize Him, considering they, too, had material senses like ours?'

The *Yajur Veda* provides the answer:

>*tasya no rāsva tasya no dhehī*

'Only when one is anointed by the nectar of the grace of the Supreme Lord, can one see Him.'

The granting of spiritual vision is an act of grace by God. He adds His divine eyes to the soul's material eyes; He provides His divine mind to the soul's material mind; He imbues His divine intellect to the soul's material intellect. Only then can the soul see the Supreme, know Him, and love Him.

Some inquire: 'How can we receive God's grace?' We have to surrender to Him, which means that we must unite our mind with Him in devotion, as Soordas did.

God Writes for Soordas and His Last Days

Soordas had resolved to write 125,000 padas. He wrote a significant number when he realized his time was up. Shree Krishna was beckoning him to return to His abode. The Sage's body had grown weak, and he too desired to return to his Beloved Lord. Yet, he also wanted to finish the remaining poems and fulfil his undertaking.

Some believe that Shree Krishna intervened. To fulfil the wish of His pure devotee, He wrote the outstanding padas, *thereby* bringing the total to 125,000. *This explains why some* padas *have the pseudonym Soor, while others are signed Soor Shyam. The ones where Shree Krishna wrote for Soordas, He used the pseudonym Soor Shyam.*

A while later, the Mughal Emperor Akbar ordered a compilation of Soordas' padas*. However, by then many impostors had also written* padas *under Soordas' name. Hence, the compilation amounted to a staggering 250,000* padas*. Consequently, Akbar proposed a test to check for their authenticity. He ordered all the* padas *to be thrown into a lake, declaring that the genuine ones would float. Remarkably, only 20,000* padas *stayed buoyant, confirming their legitimacy, while the others got submerged. Of these, very few are available today.*

On his last day, Soordas did not go for his usual darshan and service of Shrinathji. In the temple, devotees got the premonition that the Lord had refused to eat, so they grew anxious. Vitthalnathji, who used to be the temple priest, declared, 'A big ship of the Pushti Marg Sampradaya is about to depart today.'

Hearing this, everyone went to have their final darshan of Soordas and gathered around him. One of them requested, 'You have sung many *padas* for Radha Krishna, but none for your Guru.'

Soordas responded, 'Everything I sang was in the service of my Guru. It was his command that guided me.' He then composed one final poem:

>śrī vallabh nakh chandra chhaṭā binu,
>   sab jag māhiṅ andhero

'Without the light emanating from the nails of my Gurudev's lotus feet, the whole world is dark and grim.'

This was his last composition. People understood it was time for the great Sage to leave the world. Soordas was lying on his back on the sacred earth of Braj. He requested the devotees to turn him over to lie on his stomach so that his face would look towards the holy land. Offering obeisance, with loving absorption to Radha Krishna, Soordas departed from the world. Historians estimate his disappearance between 1561–63 CE, while others declare it around 1580–84 CE.

Soordas—an Incarnation of Uddhav

The *Bhaktamal* is a revered scripture by Saint Nabha Das. In it, he chronicles the life histories of many saints. Nabha Das states that Soordas was an incarnation of Uddhav, a close confidant of Shree Krishna. Uddhav was not only Krishna's dear friend but also His trusted minister in Mathura.

Krishna once confided to Uddhav, *Udho Mohin Braj Bisarat Nahi*, expressing His inability to forget Braj. Uddhav, being a worshipper of the formless and a jnani, gently chastised Krishna for His deep attachment to the gopis.

At this point, Shree Krishna sent Uddhav to meet the gopis to reveal the glories of divine love. The conversation between them is known as the *Uddhav-Gopi Samvad*.

Uddhav went to Vrindavan with the intention of giving them knowledge. His message was, 'You should not yearn for God. You yourselves are the Supreme Entity, and everywhere is Brahman.'

The gopis patiently listened to Uddhav's dissertation of jnana yog. When he finished, they revealed their own elevated state of God-realization. They expressed to him their deep absorption in Shyamsundar, regarding Him as their very life-airs.

Uddhav was astonished at the elevated state of the gopis. He was consequently graced by them with divine love and became immersed in bhakti. When he returned to Mathura, he fell at the feet of Shree Krishna, expressing his deep gratitude for the association with the gopis. He then asked the Lord for a boon:

'O Shree Krishna, these gopis have attained the state that even the greatest mystics have not. I yearn to become eligible for their grace. I will consider it my greatest good fortune to be born in my next life as a creeper, a bush, or a tree in Vrindavan so that I may receive their foot dust.' (Bhagavatam 10.47.61)

Uddhav spent his remaining days near Kusum Sarovar in the land of Govardhan, immersed in divine love and singing the glories of Radha Krishna.

Nabha Dasji describes that Shree Krishna gave Uddhav the boon of propagating the fame of gopis' love in Kaliyug. Though blind, he would be endowed with clairvoyance and musical talent that would enable him to perceive God's Leelas with his inner eyes and sing them to his heart's content.

Compositions and Literature

Soordas' legacy endures, and his literary compositions continue to be a significant portion of the Indian devotional canon. He is best known for his magnum opus, the *Soor Sagar* (Ocean of Melody). It vividly describes the loving pastimes of Radha

Krishna; the intense longing of Radha and the gopis for Shree Krishna in periods of separation; and the loving childhood Leelas of the Lord.

The *Soor Sagar* also includes the poet's personal praises for the Lord and his devotional sentiments, along with episodes from the Ramayan and Mahabharat.

Soordas was an outstanding proponent of Shree Krishna *prem*. He expressed the supremacy of bhakti for attaining spiritual perfection and further expounded it as the easiest path to fulfil the soul's hankering for Bhagavan. His devotion was devoid of ostentatious rules or stern austerities. His life and works have left a permanent imprint on Indian spirituality for centuries to come.

4

Tukaram

Tukaram was a prominent Marathi Saint of the seventeenth century. During his short life, Tukaram emphasized inner transformation and ethical living over ritualistic practices. He saw God in every being. However, his innocence often made him a target for deception and humiliation in interactions with the public. Despite enduring a life of poverty and severe hardships, his faith never faltered. He worshipped Panduranga Vitthal Dev, the presiding Krishna deity in the famous Vitthal Rukmini (Rakhumai) temple in Pandharpur. Tukaram perceived Their divine grace in every situation of his life.

Tukaram was renowned for his devotional poetry, known as *abhangas*. These short poems are characterized by their simplicity and imbue a profound personal connection with Bhagavan Vitthal, also known as Panduranga. Simply hearing these devotional hymns can purify the heart and awaken one's innate love for God. This led to their widespread popularity and profound influence on Marathi literature. Tukaram's *abhangas* continue to be sung in homes and temples across Maharashtra. Simple villagers and learned scholars alike savour them for their sweet devotional bliss.

Tukaram was instrumental in shaping the devotional *Varkari* tradition. The *Varkari Yatra* is a famous pilgrimage undertaken by lakhs of devotees in June–July every year. As an expression of their devotion to Rukmini Vithoba, pilgrims walk barefoot to Pandharpur, from all over Maharashtra and neighbouring states.

Comfortable Childhood to an Impoverished Youth

Tukaram was born in 1608 in Dehu, a small village on the banks of the Indrayani River, near Pune, Maharashtra. His father, Bolhoba, and mother, Kankara More, were devotees of Bhagavan Vitthal. The spiritual environment at home helped nurture Tukaram's devotion from a young age.

Bolhoba was a prosperous farmer and trader. Thus, Tukaram had an affluent childhood, along with his elder brother, Savaji, and younger brother, Kanhoba. When Bolhoba grew old, he asked Savaji to take charge of the business. But Savaji was disinterested in worldly pursuits. Consequently, the father turned to Tukaram, who accepted the task. Though he was yet a teenager, Tukaram earned everyone's admiration for his competent handling of the family business.

Destiny, however, had other plans. Tukaram lost his parents when he was just 17. This was soon followed by the death of Savaji's wife. Savaji then became a sanyasi and left home. At the same time, the business suffered a downturn, and despite toiling day and night, Tukaram found himself losing money. Nevertheless, he remained honest in his dealings and never cheated his customers. Eventually, Tukaram became impoverished. But this was not the end of his woes. Tragedy struck once again as a devastating famine, and Tukaram's first wife, Rakhabai, and son passed away.

Usually, in the face of such immense suffering, people stagger in their belief. Pointing a finger towards God, they question: 'Why did He do this to me?' They expect God to be an order supplier, Who should be at their beck and call to fulfil their tiniest wishes.

Tukaram's devotion, however, never wavered. Such steadfastness in faith, in the face of life's trials, is the hallmark of great souls. During hardships, they become even more firm in their belief and fervent in their love. This can be compared to a young sapling that has not been watered for three days. Its roots dig deeper to find the water so critical for survival. Similarly, the faith of Saints grows stronger during challenging times as they remind themselves of the various ways in which God has blessed them in the past. It is this faith and devotion that the Lord reciprocates abundantly.

Blessing From God and Guru

The series of reversals strengthened Tukaram's conviction about the ephemeral nature of the material realm. His already detached mind developed stark dispassion towards worldly affairs. The consequence was that his devotion to Bhagavan Panduranga intensified.

Tukaram often retreated in solitude to Brahmagiri, a mountain near Dehu, where he poured out his heart in intense prayer to the Lord. In one of his *abhangas*, he recounts the venomous bites from snakes and scorpions there. Yet, he remained undeterred in his devotion, and eventually, Vitthal Bhagavan gave him darshan. Tukaram humbly held the lotus feet of his Lord and poured out his deepest devotional sentiments. Lord Panduranga then blessed him with the art of composing and singing poetry.

A while later, Tukaram also had a vision of Chaitanya Mahaprabhu in a dream. Mahaprabhu accepted Tukaram as his disciple and instructed him to propagate the divine Names of God—Ram, Krishna, and Hari. Tukaram describes this in one of his *abhangas*:

> *sadguru-rāye kṛipā maza kelī*
> *pari nāhī ghaḍalī sevā kāhī* ||1||
> *sāpaḍvile vāte zātā gangāsnānā*
> *mastakī to zāṇā ṭhevilā kara* ||2||

'A Sadhguru appeared before me when I was on my way to bathe in the river. Even though I didn't know how to serve him, he blessed me by placing his hand on my head.'

Tukaram was, thus, doubly blessed by God and Guru. In Their service, he flooded the entire state of Maharashtra with kirtan, the congregational singing of the Lord's names. His philosophy was simple: Chant the Names of God. There is no need to renounce your household life, rather, integrate God into every aspect of it. Surrendering to Him is the most potent form of devotion. Do not get entangled in elaborate rituals. Instead, the easiest form of bhakti is remembering the Names of God.

Tukaram composed countless poems with the sole aim of glorifying the Supreme. He sang them during his frequent pilgrimages from Dehu to Pandharpur. His melodious chanting inspired hundreds to join these holy pada yatras for darshan at the Shri Vitthal Rukmini temple. Together, they would sing, dance, and play musical instruments throughout the journey, covering distances of up to 300 kilometres.

This simple yet powerful tradition gave rise to the *Varkari Yatra*—a movement that thrives even today. Throughout the procession, devotees disregard personal hardships and continue singing Tukaram's *abhangas* and other Marathi kirtans. The *varkaris* carry *padukas* (sandals) of Saint Tukaram and other revered saints of Maharashtra in decorated palanquins during their yatra.

Signs of Divinity

Tukaram's *abhangas* provoked the wrath of the local brahmins. They were indignant that Tukaram had encroached on their authority by simplifying the teachings of the Gita in his *abhangas*. Feeling threatened by his growing influence, they connived to preserve their societal dominance.

One local brahmin, Rameshwar Bhatt, accosted Tukaram in front of a gathering. He questioned Tukaram's authority in composing the *abhangas* and alleged that a non-brahmin and non-scholar was corrupting their religion. He claimed it was incorrect to disseminate scriptural knowledge in a common language like Marathi instead of Sanskrit. Tukaram, in all his humility, responded through an *abhanga*:

> kariton kavitva mhaṇāla he koṇhī
> navhe mājhī vāṇī padarīchī ||1||
> mājhiye yuktīchā navhe hā prakāra
> maza viśvambhara bolavīto ||2||

> *kāya mī pāmara zāṇe arthabheda*
> *vadavī govinda techi vadeṅ* ||3||

'You may say that I compose poems, but they are not my words. It is not my own creation but inspiration from the universal Creator. I am but a small and unimportant person, without any capability. It is the Divine who empowers my speech.'

Tukaram's logic, however, did not convince Rameshwar Bhatt, who blamed him for making excuses. Tukaram bowed down to the scholarly brahmin community and accepted their verdict that he had committed a religious transgression. He asked what atonement he must do. Rameshwar directed him to throw the manuscripts of his *abhangas* into the Indrayani River. In sarcasm, he also challenged that if Tukaram was a true devotee, the manuscripts would reappear themselves.

On hearing this instruction, Tukaram was heartbroken. He had written the *abhangas* in the loving service of Rukmini Vitthal. Now he was being asked to atone for his sin by rejecting them all. Nevertheless, wiping away his tears, he threw them into the river. Then he sat under a tree and fervently cried out the Lord's Name since kirtan was the only way known to him.

Thirteen days later, the manuscripts were found floating on the water. Retrieving them, someone brought them to Tukaram, who was still sitting under the tree, immersed in kirtan. The Saint was overjoyed on being reunited with his *abhangas* manuscripts. Even more satisfying was the divine sign that Panduranga had accepted his devotional compositions.

The message was loud and clear—by revealing Vedic knowledge in Marathi, Tukaram had not committed any crime. The news that Vitthal Bhagavan had endorsed the *abhangas* spread like wildfire. After this miraculous event, the villagers acknowledged Tukaram's sanctity. Even Rameshwar Bhatt, realizing his mistake, apologized to the God-empowered Saint.

Struggles of Married Life

Tukaram's second marriage was with Jijabai. Being materialistically inclined, she could not understand her husband's other-worldly ways. While the entire village revered Tukaram as a saint, Jijabai thought of him merely as someone to whom she was betrothed. She was known for her nagging nature.

One day, Tukaram saw Jijabai worshipping Mother Lakshmi. Jijabai explained that devotion to the goddess of wealth would help them alleviate poverty. Tukaram disagreed with her intention, saying it was tainted with an ulterior motive, and hence, it was not pure devotion.

'Why not?' Jijabai argued. 'You worship Vishnu, the Husband. I worship Lakshmi, His wife. How can this be wrong?'

A few days later, Jijabai got some money and equipped their home with necessities. She credited it to Mother Lakshmi's grace. Hearing this, Tukaram walked out of the house. Jijabai was accustomed to her husband leaving home for a day or two to engage in kirtan. However, this time many days passed, and he did not return.

Jijabai was now very worried. As the wife of a saint, she received a special blessing. Panduranga Bhagavan appeared in her dream and showed her Tukaram's location. Following the directions, Jijabai climbed atop the hill and reached the revealed spot.

There, she found her husband absorbed in kirtans—he had been sitting there without food for days.

Jijabai urged him to return home. Tukaram retorted, 'Now that you have Mother Lakshmi's grace in the house, why do you need me?'

Although Jijabai was quarrelsome, she was a chaste woman with a strong sense of duty to her husband. Wailing with emotion, she clarified that her husband meant more to her than all the wealth in the world. Tukaram then made her promise that she would not ask for material boons while doing bhakti. In addition, whatever she could save at home, she would donate to the needy. Tukaram was convinced that the Lord would provide for their needs, and therefore, they should not hesitate to serve others. Jijabai accepted all conditions, and Tukaram returned home with her.

Clearly Tukaram's only interest was in serving his Vitthal Bhagavan, and he was willing to go to any lengths for it. According to the scriptures, bhakti should be *nishkām* (selfless), *ananya* (exclusive), and *nirantar* (continuous). Tukaram exemplified these three criteria as he showed that if one has God by his side, then one has everything. This is just as placing the number 'one' before a 'zero'. A 'one' at the end of any number of zeros will always mean 'one'. On the other hand, when placed before a zero or any number of zeros, it changes the value exponentially.

Bhagavan in Service of His Devotee's Servitor

Tukaram's constant immersion in kirtan and neglect of his

worldly duties frustrated Jijabai. She would vent her emotions by blaming Bhagavan Vitthal for leading her husband astray. Sometimes, inflamed in anger, she even mocked the Lord, calling Him *Ittu* (the Deity that stands on a brick).

Yet, Jijabai remained a dutiful wife; irrespective of where Tukaram was, she would always personally bring him his meals. On one such occasion of walking barefoot, a thorn pierced Jijabai's foot. She screamed in pain.

Unexpectedly someone came and addressing her as 'mother', gently plucked the thorn from her foot. Relieved, Jijabai inquired his name. The man replied with a smile, 'I am *Ittu*', and vanished.

When Jijabai recounted the incident to Tukaram, he realized that only Bhagavan Vitthal could have come at such an opportune time. Overcome with emotion, he wept thinking how causelessly merciful God was. From that day on, Tukaram made it a point to return home for his meals, not wanting the Lord of the universe to take pains for him.

Bhagavan Comes to the Rescue

Tukaram lived during the reign of Chhatrapati Shivaji Maharaj. Shivaji was astounded by the Saint's attitude of renunciation despite his abject poverty. The Maratha king offered Tukaram some gold to ease his hardships.

Tukaram saw the gold and began trembling. He quickly got up and left the room. Confused by the Saint's behaviour, Shivaji asked the disciples what had happened. They explained that Gurudev hated being tempted by wealth. Nevertheless, Shivaji persisted. He requested Tukaram to accept the offering in the organization of his satsang and pilgrimages.

Tukaram replied, 'You have known me only for a short time and are worried about me. Think how concerned Panduranga must be for me. He has known me not only from birth but also in previous lives too.'

Shivaji was speechless. He tried again, insisting the Saint accept the offering for the pleasure of Shivaji. Tukaram silenced him with this logic: 'If you offer me beef, and request that I consume it for your happiness, will I eat it just to please you? Similarly, to me, your wealth is like the flesh of a cow.'

Realizing that he could not succeed in convincing the Saint, Shivaji withdrew his request.

On another occasion, it was Ekadashi and Shivaji was relishing Tukaram's kirtan. The king was dressed in plain clothes to avoid detection by his Mughal enemies. Unfortunately, Shivaji's whereabouts were shared with a Mughal commander who sent two thousand soldiers to capture and kill Shivaji. Shivaji's spies got wind of the enemy plan and reported the precarious matter to their king. They suggested he depart immediately.

When Shivaji sought Tukaram's permission to leave, the Saint instructed him to stay and continue the satsang. Shivaji was now in a quandary. Nevertheless, he obeyed the Saint's instruction and left it to the will of God. He would either be saved by divine grace or willingly die in sacred association.

Strangely, though the enemy soldiers reached the place, they could not spot Shivaji amongst the devotees. The Mughal commander ordered the massacre of the entire assembly as he was sure of Shivaji's presence in it. The soldiers surrounded the devotee congregation.

At that very moment, they spotted a rider, looking exactly like Shivaji, on a horseback, galloping away. Presuming him to be the Maratha king, the Mughal army chased the rider. He led them a long distance away, and then mysteriously disappeared. The bewildered Mughal commander could not comprehend how two thousand soldiers failed to capture a single man.

When the incident was reported to Tukaram, he revealed the secret. Bhagavan Panduranga had come on horseback in the guise of Shivaji, to mislead the Mughal army and protect the satsang. Shivaji's faithful surrender to the instructions of Tukaram obliged the Lord to personally intervene and shield him.

A famous Bengali saying goes: *rākhe krishna māre ke, māre krishna rākhe ke*. In essence, it implies that when God decides to protect one, then who can harm him? Similarly, if the Lord decides one's time on earth is over, then no doctor or medicine can save one. In the face of the Divine's will, even the mightiest force and most powerful weapons are rendered useless.

Simplicity of the Heart

One particular year, the rains failed, and a severe drought gripped Dehu. To earn some money and meet ends for his family, Tukaram set out with bags of chillies towards Konkan. Throughout his journey, the name of Rukmini Vitthal stayed on his lips.

On reaching from the seacoast, Tukaram spread his wares on the ground and sat down there thinking about the form of Panduranga. Villagers soon gathered around, asking about the prices. The unconcerned Tukaram told them to take whatever they wanted at the usual price. The customers filled the measure themselves. Tukaram, absorbed in his devotional thoughts, didn't bother to check or note how much each person was taking.

The news spread through the village, and people flocked to buy chillies. Tukaram agreed to purchases of handfuls, *maunds*, and even an entire sack of chillies on credit. Tukaram trusted everyone without any qualms.

In no time, all the sacks were empty. Feeling relieved that his business was done, Tukaram began cooking some rice, lost in thoughts of the Divine. Meanwhile, a stranger arrived in that village. Introducing himself as Tukaram's representative, he requested everyone for the money they owed for the chillies. Most people denied on the pretext of not remembering their measure. However, the stranger told them precisely how much each one had taken. Stupefied, all the villagers quickly paid up. The stranger handed over the collected sum to the Saint, and then quietly departed.

Tukaram, assuming the man was the village watchman, didn't give it much thought. Later, when the villagers came to meet Tukaram, they discovered that he had not sent anyone to collect his debts. Realizing what had transpired, Tukaram, with a heart overflowing with gratitude, simply said, 'Unfathomable are the ways of Hari!'

The Quintessential Expression of Gratitude

One day, amid the lack of basic necessities at home, Jijabai gave Tukaram her jewellery to mortgage for money. Returning home with the cash, Tukaram encountered beggars and street children. Overcome with compassion, he distributed all the money in charity. Beholding him come home empty-handed, Jijabai's heart sank in despair.

Seeing his wife's distress, Tukaram was deeply pained and set out in search of a job outside. He knew that in Dehu village everyone revered him and would not employ him. So, he went to a nearby village where a farmer agreed to hire him. The villager had heard of Tukaram but never seen him. Unaware of whom he had employed, he assigned the work of protecting the crop from birds. The farmer then left for a month.

Even while working in the field, Tukaram remained absorbed in contemplation of Bhagavan Panduranga. He saw the birds pecking the grain but perceived them as the Lord's creatures. So, he allowed them to feast sumptuously from the very field he was supposed to guard. When the farmer returned a month later, and found the crop ravaged, he was furious. He reprimanded Tukaram severely and demanded a compensation of Rs. 2000 for the loss incurred under his vigilance.

Though Tukaram had taken the job to solve his financial problems, they had now multiplied. Calling the Lord to show the way, Tukaram exclaimed, 'O Panduranga!'

The farmer mocked him for imitating the famous Saint Tukaram. When Tukaram admitted his identity, the farmer was shocked. He had unwittingly engaged the great Saint in petty work. Filled with penitence, he begged pardon from Tukaram. Thanking the Saint for sanctifying his field with his feet, he gifted a cart full of sugarcane to Tukaram.

The news that Tukaram had received the generous gift reached Jijabai. She sent a message to him to sell the sugarcane for money so that they could purchase some household essentials.

On his way home, some children saw the Saint with the cartful of sugarcane. Eager to enjoy God's delicacy, they began chanting 'Panduranga Panduranga', hoping to please Tukaram. Moved by their innocent devotion, Tukaram distributed all the sugarcane to the children and returned home with just one piece.

Jijabai's forbearance had reached its limit. She took the sugarcane and hit it on her husband's head. It broke into two. However, Tukaram retained his composure, like only a Saint can, and suggested, 'Glad it has split. You take one half, and I will take the other.'

Tukaram subsequently went to the local temple and thanked Bhagavan Panduranga for the harsh experience. By giving him a brutal wife, the Lord had ensured that he would never get enmeshed in worldly attachments. He recognized this hardship as the Almighty's unique blessing.

We must learn this ability from the Saints. When adversity befalls them, they choose to look at the silver lining. They firmly believe that every opportunity can be utilized for learning and the soul's evolution. This is the fine art of 'positive reframing'.

How we choose to see the world is a choice we make. Misery is the consequence of viewing life through the lens of negativity and discontentment. Conversely, positive reframing involves finding the bright side in any situation and then focusing upon it.

Much of this world and its events are out of our control. Anxiety attacks us because we are attached to how things 'should be' versus how 'they are'. Deficiencies that we cannot change repeatedly come to our mind. This results in discontentment, which becomes the cause for misery. The reverse is acceptance of things beyond our power. Sage Narad recommends the same mindset:

loka-hānau chintā na kāryā niveditātma-loka-vedatvāt

(*Narad Bhakti Darshan*, sutra 61)

'If worldly calamity befalls, do not become anxious. Instead, choose to see God's grace in it.'

From our perspective, pain is a bad thing, while pleasure is most desirable. Contrarily, the Vedas guide us to make self-growth our goal and not the maximization of pleasure. The perspective of self-improvement empowers us to see grace in both good and bad situations. In fact, the Vedic scriptures go a step further and tell us the whole world is the veritable form of God. The *Ishavasya Upanishad* states:

īśhā vāsyam-idam sarvam yat-kiñcha jagatyām jagat

'All that exists in the universe is a manifestation of the Supreme Lord.' The Bhagavad Gita states:

vāsudevaḥ sarvam iti (verse 7.19)

'The Supreme Lord is all that is.' And Sage Tulsidas states in the Ramayan:

sīyā rāmamay sab jag jānī, karauñ pranām jori jug pānī

(verse 1.7.1)

'The whole world is full of the presence of Sita Ram. Hence, I fold my hands and offer my respects to all.'

All these scriptures reiterate that the world created by God is auspicious and divine. We must get out of our tunnel vision and adopt new ways of reasoning based on higher wisdom. The shift in perspective will release us from the shackles of despair.

So, the next time you feel anxious or depressed, simply change your viewpoint, and the door to happiness will magically open. It does not require an external key.

Teachings and Inspirations

The central theme of Tukaram's teachings was to live a life of devotion and service. This means that we consider ourselves as the soul. Keeping in mind that the soul is a servant of the Supreme Soul, all activities of one's daily life should be dedicated to the Lord. In this *abhanga*, he urges people to recount the various visible graces in their life.

kaṅ re nāṭhavīsī kṛipāḻu devāsī
　posito janāsī ekalā to ||1||
bāḻā dudhā koṇa kariteṅ utpattī
　vāḍhavī shrīpatī saveṅ donhī ||2||
phuṭati tarūvara ushṇ-kāḻ-māsiṅ
　jīvana tayānsī koṇa ghālī ||3||
teṇeṅ tujhī kāya nāhīṅ kelī chintā
　rāheṅ tyāṅ anantā āṭhavūnī ||4||
tukā mhaṇe jyāche ñāva vishvambhara
　tyāche nirantara dhyana karīṅ ||5||

'How can you forget the merciful God, who sustains everything in the world? He is the one who infuses life in a newborn and also provides nourishing milk through the mother. God is the one sustaining both mother and child. Trees grow even in the hot summer season; Who provides them with life-sustaining water? Live in constant remembrance of God, Who fulfils all your needs. That infinite God pervades the entire universe; remember Him every moment.'

Since the scriptures explain that God's Name is more powerful than God Himself, Tukaram emphasized *naam* kirtan, or the congregational chanting of the divine Names of God. He also encouraged devotees towards the selfless service of humankind, rather than elaborate rituals. He vehemently opposed the acquisition of yogic siddhis (mystical abilities), for they led to pride and obstructed authentic sadhana.

Saint Tukaram did not favour the display of asceticism or preoccupation with austerities. On these, he retorted, 'Even dogs come in saffron colour, and bears have matted fur. If living in caves is being spiritual, then rats who inhabit caves must be doing sadhana (spiritual practice).'

The Saint urged people to abandon customs that hindered devotion. Instead, he exhorted them to put God at the centre of their life and see Him in all beings. In one of his *abhangas*, Tukaram critiques the mechanical ritual of visiting pilgrimages and taking dips in holy waters:

jāūniyāṅ tirthā kāya tuvāṅ keleṅ
   charma prakṣhāḷileṅ varīṅ varīṅ ||1||
antarīnche śhuddha kāsayāneṅ jāleṅ
   bhuṣhṇa tvāṅ keln āpaṇayā ||2||

vṛindāvan-phala gholileṅ sākarā
bhītarīla ṭhārā modechinā ||3||
tukā mhaṇe nāhīṅ śhānti kṣhamā dayā
tonvarī kāsayā phundā tumhī ||4||

'Of what value is the visit of holy places, merely to cleanse the outside dirt on the body? Such acts may enhance your external appearance, but does it purify your heart? A bitter fruit coated with sugar outside continues to remain bitter inside. Tukaram says you will never have peace of mind without piety, compassion, and forgiveness.'

During his frequent pilgrimages from Dehu to Pandharpur, Tukaram used his *abhangas* to emphasize the code of conduct for the *varkaris*. This included good moral behaviour and respect for all, regardless of caste, creed, and wealth. He engaged people in service of the poor by providing them food and other basic necessities. Serving God's creation, he felt, was the way to serve God. These teachings continue to be upheld in present-day *varkari* yatras.

Tukaram was an epitome of compassion. In fact, after his father's death and the collapse of his family business, he faced extreme poverty, yet his kindness did not deplete. He even destroyed the records of loans his father had made to the poor and waived off their debts permanently.

Poetic Compositions

Due to a lack of formal education and training on this path, Tukaram sought guidance by studying the works of renowned Saints from his homeland, such as Jnaneshwar, Namdev, and Eknath. The result was more than 4500 *abhangas* in Marathi, which have been compiled in the *Tukaram Gatha*.

Abhanga is a type of devotional poetry, meaning 'an unflawed and perpetual procedure'. It symbolizes the continuous chanting by devotees, as an expression of exclusive love for Bhagavan Panduranga. Tukaram was unparalleled in his mastery of this poetic form.

While Tukaram was a master par excellence in the *abhangas* style of kirtans, he also composed verses in other forms, such as aarti, *gaulani*, and shloka. And though most of his compositions are predominantly in Marathi, some works can be found in Hindi as well.

Despite the fact that Tukaram was not a great scholar, the depth of his understanding of the world and human nature was evident. His compositions, covering hundreds of themes, vividly depict the state of society, religion, and the nation during his time. Tukaram's straightforward poetry made wisdom accessible to ordinary people and resonated deeply with them so much so that lines from many of his *abhangas* have become household sayings in the state of Maharashtra.

Samadhi

In 1650, Tukaram received a divine indication that it was time for him to depart from the mortal plane. He spent that entire night singing his *abhangas*, absorbed in bhakti.

It is widely believed that a magnificent celestial chariot descended from the spiritual realm for Tukaram. Other versions suggest that Garud, Bhagavan Vishnu's mount, personally arrived to escort him. In front of everyone's eyes, singing the praises of the Lord, Tukaram ascended to the spiritual realm.

Today, a shrine dedicated to Tukaram stands in Pandharpur, where devotees offer their homage to him during the *Varkari Yatra*.

5
Kabirdas

Saint Kabir appeared in fifteenth century India. He belonged to the first wave of saints in the Bhakti Movement, even before Tulsidas, Soordas, Gaurang Mahaprabhu, and Meerabai. Kabir did not follow the conventional path of a monk. He hailed from the weaver community and worked hard to make ends meet. However, his mind was always absorbed in the Divine, and thus, he exemplified a true karm yogi. Although Kabir was not formally educated, he was unsuppressable in his wisdom and bold in his expressions.

In those medieval times, Indian religious ethos had a heavy focus on external acts, such as reading loud religious prayers and performing mechanical poojas. The emphasis on cultivation of inner sentiments was missing. Bhakti was ostentatious, while adherence to dharma was limited to observing empty rituals. Discrimination based on caste, status, and religion was a common social malady. Amidst the social chaos and drama, the simple path of selfless love for God had been sidelined.

Kabir challenged societal divisions and meaningless rituals by employing satire and irony in his pithy poems. He sought to spread a religion of love to unite people of all castes and religions. Thus, he strived to reconstruct people's spiritual experience for social harmony.

Kabir was the first saint to reconcile Hindus and Muslims on mutual tenets of spirituality. He urged common people to look beyond superficial differences in religious practices and connect with the Divine within. As a result, in the annals of history, Kabir's name is etched as a religious reformer and an icon of social renaissance.

As a Bhakti poet, Kabir ushered in a revival of spiritual fervour amongst the masses. At a time when Sanskrit and Persian were the languages of religious discourses, Kabir composed couplets in Hindi mixed with local languages—Avadhi, Braj, Khari boli, Bhojpuri, Punjabi, Rajasthani, and Urdu—making them highly accessible to common people. His short compositions, sprinkled with colloquial idioms, presented universal lessons on human nature. He liberally shared wisdom on the purpose of human life and the essence of spirituality in a way palatable to the masses.

No wonder, even today, people readily quote 'Kabir ke Dohe'. His teachings significantly impact across religious cultures in India. Hence, he is universally respected by Hindus, Muslims, and Sikhs.

Discovery of the Name 'Kabir'

There are different stories regarding the birth of Kabir. The most popular version states that his mother was a devout brahmin maiden. Out of fear of ill-repute, she left her infant under a bridge. The baby was discovered by a poor childless couple, Noor Ali and Neema Jaan. They brought him home and raised him with great love and affection, amidst their community of weavers.

During the naming ceremony, the baby was taken to a maulvi (Muslim priest). As per the tradition, the maulvi randomly opened a page of the Quran to check for a name. The word *Kabir* surfaced, which means 'great' and symbolizes God. The maulvi dismissed it as an accident. He reopened the Quran several times, and every time the word *Kabir* appeared. Considering this as the will of the Almighty, the baby was named Kabir.

As an infant, Kabir refused to accept the food that his parents tried to feed him. Someone then advised the parents to feed only vegetarian food to the special child. History bears witness that even though Kabir was brought up in a Muslim house, he remained vegetarian all his life. The Kabir Chaura locality in Kashi is believed to be the place where he spent most of his life.

When Kabir was admitted in a madrasa to study, he never paid heed to formal learning. He was interested only in the name of Ram. He was convinced that the one who knows the Supreme, knows everything of importance in this world.

Hardships in Daily Life

Kabir grew up in poverty and spent his entire life in scarcity. When he entered youth, his father passed away, and the responsibility of the household fell on Kabir's shoulders. He took to his father's profession of weaving. He weaved cloth on a loom and worked hard for a living. However, these hardships never deterred him from meditating upon God.

Kabir married a woman named Loi. Together, they had a son,

Kamal, and a daughter, Kamali. By his own example, he showed that one does not need to abandon worldly life and reside in seclusion. Rather, Kabir advocated integrating awareness of God in every strand of life. In his own words:

> prem bhāv ek chāhiye, bhes anek banāy
> chāhe ghar meṅ vās kar, chāhe van meṅ jāy

'If you have love for God in your heart, it does not matter what you wear, or where you stay—at home or in the forest.'

Kabir exemplified the ideal of simple living and high thinking. Weaving was not only his profession but also an expression of his devotion to God. His poetry abounds in weaving metaphors; hence, he gained the title: 'the weaver of God's Name'.

Getting Accepted by the Guru

Kabir aspired to have a Guru in his life. Kabir's mind was attracted to Swami Ramananda, who was a famous Guru. He was the founder of the Ramananda sect that continues even today.

Swami Ramananda adhered to Vedic processes of devotion, diligently observing all rituals. Complying with the social norms of his era, Swami Ramananda was initially unwilling to meet Kabir due to his lineage. But Kabir, unwavering in his determination, ingeniously devised a plan to be accepted as Gurudev's disciple.

Kabir discovered that each day Swami Ramananda went to bathe in the sacred Ganga in Kashi, around Brahma Muhurt, i.e., at approximately 4.00 a.m. So, Kabir seized this opportunity and deliberately lay on the stairs leading to the Ganga ghat.

Swami Ramananda came walking down the stairs. In the

dark, he accidentally stepped on Kabir, and exclaimed 'Ram, Ram' in apology. Kabir was overjoyed. He regarded this as an initiation by his Guru. Such was his devotional fervour for his Spiritual Master!

In his *dohas*, Kabir has repeatedly emphasized the significance of a Guru.

> *guru govind doū khaḍe, kāke lāgū pāy*
> *balihārī guru āpane, govind diyo batāy*

The verse is a question Kabir asks himself. 'Guru and God are both standing before me. To whom should I offer my obeisance first? Let me first bow at the feet of my Guru, for by his grace, I could meet God.'

Kabir's guru bhakti impressed Swami Ramananda. He accepted Kabir as his disciple. However, he would not allow Kabir to sit in front of him. Maintaining a distance from the lower strata of society, Swami Ramananda would converse with Kabir through a curtain. But this soon changed.

One day, Swami Ramananda was busy with his usual rituals of worshipping the deity of Shree Ram. He had adorned the crown. But when he tried to place the garland, it was too small to go over the crown. Swami Ramananda was perplexed by the lapse in his daily routine.

Kabir, sitting on the other side of the curtain, promptly spoke, 'Gurudev, please remove the crown and put the garland. Then you can adorn the crown again on Shree Ram.'

Swami Ramananda was deeply impressed with the divine vision of his new disciple. He tore the curtain apart and embraced him. Thenceforth, Kabir became a close adviser to his Guru.

Usually, a disciple learns from his Guru, but in Kabir's case, the reverse was also true. His thoughts helped Swami Ramananda broaden his own perspectives. He, therefore, later accepted Ravidas and Dhanna Jaat as his disciples, who also belonged to the lower strata of society.

Extraordinary Feats

A learned pandit, Sarvajit, once came to meet Kabir. He was a well-versed scholar who loved engaging in debates with people to prove his superiority. In the arrogance of his learnedness, Sarvajit arrived at Kabir's residence in a bullock cart that was laden with books. Kabir admitted that he had never even seen such a stockpile of books earlier. When Sarvajit invited him for debate, Kabir said it was not required. He was willing to admit defeat without it.

Sarvajit was delighted but sought a written confession of defeat. He asked Kabir to sign a note that read, 'Sarvajit defeated Kabir'. Kabir signed it without a fuss.

Sarvajit returned home and displayed the letter to his mother, claiming he had proof he had vanquished Kabir in debate. However, when she read the note, it stated, 'Kabir defeated Sarvajit'.

Sarvajit was perplexed. He went back to Kabir and wrote the same message again on a fresh paper. Once more, Kabir signed it without any dispute. Again, when the mother read the note, the message had reversed. This episode repeated a few times until the wise mother explained to her ignorant son that his arrogance could never vanquish Kabir's humility. The pursuit of fame had made Sarvajit blind to the impurities of his own mind. On the contrary, the depth of Kabir's realized wisdom was evident in his simplicity.

Pride subtly fosters a bloated and arrogant perception of the self. Consequently, it clouds our intellect, creating grandiose self-opinions. Possession of wealth, beauty, knowledge, and talents inflames the ego further. We get trapped in a sense of superiority and significance in creation. In our vanity, we lose sight of God's magnificent glory. We forget that we are but tiny specks in the vast expanse of the universe. This learning is elucidated in the following example.

A rich student could not stop boasting about his massive mansion to his classmates. Overhearing this conversation, the teacher placed a map before him and asked him to identify the city in which he lived. The student pointed to a little dot.

The teacher then asked him to find his neighbourhood within the city. The student tried to mark a new dot within the previous dot.

The teacher then probed further and requested him to point out the massive mansion. It was a dot within the dot, within the dot.

Think about it. In this limitless expanse of God's creation, what do we really have to be proud of? Kabir presented the perils of pride through beautiful analogies in many couplets:

> *kabīrā garv nā kījiye, ūnchā dekh āvās*
> *kāl paḍo bhū leṭanā ūpar jamsī ghās*

Kabir says, 'Don't become proud looking at your high mansion. When death overcomes, you will be made to lie on no more than six feet of barren soil. On top of you will be the cremation grass.'

Kabir reminds us of the futility of pride and urges people to live a life of humility. In fact, humility is the quality most cherished by God, while pride is the most despised. Therefore, Kabir says:

> *jab maiṅ tha tab hari nahiṅ, ab hari hai maiṅ nāhīṅ*
> *prem galī ati sāñkarī jāme do na samāhiṅ*

'When the 'I' (ego) existed, my heart was devoid of the Divine. Now that God has entered my heart, my ego has slipped away. The path of selfless love is very narrow—it cannot accommodate two entities.'

Although Kabir is famous in the northern belt of India, a story is told about him at the holy temple of Jagannath Puri in Odisha. The temple was by the seaside. The problem, however, was that sea water often entered the temple precincts. This distressed the residents of Puri, including the king, and they deliberated on how to prevent it.

One night, Lord Jagannath Himself presented the solution. The senior priest of the temple dreamt the Lord was telling him to seek the advice of Saint Kabir, a very elevated holy soul. The next morning, the priest narrated his dream to the king. Thus, Kabir was respectfully petitioned by the royal and priestly authorities.

Kabir arrived in Jagannath Puri to survey the problem. He then sat in a boat and asked that it be taken three miles into the sea. There, he drew a line, signifying the limit of the sea's expanse. The sea receded three miles as per the demarcated line, where it is believed to be situated even today.

Defiance of Meaningless Rituals and Authorities

Once, a few brahmins were bathing in the Ganges to atone for their sins.

Kabir also entered the holy river, filled his pot with water, and offered it to them. They refused to accept it because societal norms deemed the water impure due to his touch.

Kabir retorted, 'If the holy Ganges does not have the power to purify my pot, then how can it wash away my sins and purify my soul from evil deeds?'

Through many such incidents, Kabir did not hesitate to dismantle the beliefs of the pandits and maulvis. He even rejected their priestly authority as it contributed to divisions in society.

We blindly follow many customs because of the social environment of our upbringing. We do not choose to be Brahmin, Kshatriya, Punjabi, Tamilian, Americans, or British. The location, situation, and family of our birth decide the process of our social heredity. We invariably identify ourselves with a nationality or religion or caste based upon what our parents follow, and even go to the extent of developing enmity with people of other nationalities and religions.

This happens because we consider ourselves as merely the physical body and remain engulfed in our bodily identifications. However, when we awaken to the understanding of our divine nature as fragments of the Supreme, we rise above the material designations of varna (social class). We see the same Supreme Soul equally present in all living beings. Therefore, Kabir was against observing caste hierarchies for embellishing egos. He said:

jāti na pūchho sādhu kī, pūchh lījiye jñān
mol karo talawār ka, paḍī rahan do myān

In this couplet, Kabir criticized the widespread casteism of that era by using a metaphor of the sheath and the sword. The sheath is insignificant, whereas the sword within it holds true value. Similarly, instead of enquiring about a person's caste, one should assess them based on knowledge.

Through such simple and straightforward analogies, Kabir propagated thoughts of religious and social harmony in society. He was well-versed in the human psyche and aptly addressed emotions in bold poetic messages. Pithy verses with hard-hitting words were his style of propagating the reforms required.

Once, a Qazi, Jahan Gasht Shah, set out to meet Kabir. Aware of his impending visit, Kabir tied a pig outside his hut. The Muslim tradition forbids coming in contact with pigs as they are considered unclean.

The Qazi was perturbed seeing a pig at a pious residence and chided Kabir. But Kabir remained unruffled. He responded, 'I have tied the pig outside, but you have given it shelter within your heart! Seeing the pig, your mind was filled with hatred, and it manifested on your face. The thoughts of hatred that you harboured were more impure than the pig!'

The Qazi was speechless. Kabir illuminated him by expressing that no being in God's creation should be despised. How could one claim to love God while harbouring hatred towards His creation? The only *Kafir*, or atheist, is the one who causes pain to God's children. On the other hand, the true *Momin*, or theist, is the one who loves God and sees Him in all beings. In this way, Kabir encouraged people to be virtuous in their hearts and live harmoniously with the rest of God's creation.

Deadly Opposition

Some people use Kabir's verses to condemn all rituals as adharmic. However, this was not his intent. If offering flowers, water, or food to God enhances your loving sentiments, there is no harm in using such simple aids for your bhakti. But the goal is to cultivate our love for God through the physical act of worship. The Vedic scriptures unanimously affirm the highest dharma of all souls is unconditional and ceaseless love for God. This religion of love was emphatically articulated in the following verse, which is arguably the most famous of Kabir's *dohas*:

> *pothī paḍhi paḍhi jag mua, paṇḍit bhayā na koy*
> *ḍhaī ākhar prem kā, paḍhe so paṇḍit hoy*

'Everyone reads volumes of books, yet no one became a true pandit. Only those who learn the two and half syllables of *prem* are the truly knowledgeable.'

As Kabir lacerated prominent beliefs that existed for ages, it won him many enemies. He earned the ire of Hindu and Muslim religious authorities, who accused him of blasphemy towards established religion. They complained about him to Sikandar Lodi, the then Sultan of Delhi.

Kabir was summoned to the emperor's court. The defiant Saint arrived before the powerful Sultan but refused to bow down to him. He fearlessly declared that he knew only one King, known as Allah and Bhagavan. He is the Supreme Power, and therefore, Kabir bowed only before Him.

Impressed with his irrefutable logic, Sikandar Lodi dismissed the accusations against Kabir. However, opposition to his teachings kept intensifying. So, once again, Kabir was brought to court with similar charges of disrespecting religious leaders.

This time, Sikandar Lodi succumbed to the pressure from his people. He sentenced Kabir to death by drowning. Kabir's hands and feet were bound by heavy chains, and he was unceremoniously thrown into the river. But the waves miraculously broke the chains, and he escaped. He was subsequently cast at the feet of an elephant to be pounded. Kabir, steadfast in his belief that God is omnipresent and resides even in the heart of the elephant, remained unharmed. The dumbstruck Sikandar Lodi realized that Kabir was not an ordinary being. Ashamed, he bowed before him and became his follower.

Looking at history, the question arises as to why all Saints were so vehemently opposed in their times. Not just Kabir but Meerabai, Tulsidas, Tukaram, and others were also tormented. The reason for this is evident. Saints strive for the welfare of humankind. This involves challenging prevailing beliefs and lifting people to higher levels of understanding. Unfortunately, it makes those entrenched in ignorant ways very uncomfortable. It also hurts those who are exploiting people's ignorant beliefs for their personal gain.

Besides, not everyone loves change. If you are ten steps ahead of others, they will call you a visionary. But if you are a hundred steps ahead of them, they will label you as a heretic and even kill you. This explains the opposition that Saints face in their lifetimes. How do they respond to adversities?

Saints remain equipoised in all situations—fame and infamy, praise and criticism, victory and failure. They do not lament like us. They accept dualities as an inseparable part of this world created by God, just as we accept day and night and the changing of seasons as inevitable. Likewise, when they are criticized, they accept it as the nature of the world. They leverage disparagement as an opportunity for self-purification and never permit their mind to harbour bespoiling emotions of hatred, anger, and irritation.

Teachings and Inspirations from a Commoner to the Masses

Kabir was a man of the common people. He spoke their dialect, moved with them, taught them, and lived like them. Weaving was his profession, and weaving the Divine into the human psyche and society was his life mission.

Kabir's motive was to make people contemplate the smallest pursuits in their daily living. He also confronted them with bigger questions, like the purpose of human life. Sometimes, he placed a clarion call to focus on inner transformation. In this *doha*, Kabir advises love for God over mechanical practice:

> mālā pherat jug bhayā, phirā na mana kā pher
> kar kā manakā dār de, mana kā mana kā pher

'Eons have passed twirling the rosary beads and counting its rotations as a spiritual feat, yet the state of the mind has not transformed. Now, leave the rosary aside and do something to rotate the beads of the mind.'

Kabir glorified self-sacrifice and selflessness in devotion. He stated:

> *prem na bāri upaje, prem na hāṭ bikāye*
> *rājā prajā jo hī ruche, sīs de hī le jāye*

'Divine love neither grows in the fields nor is it sold in the market. One who wants love, whether it is the king or a commoner, must pay its value by sacrificing his pride.'

Kabir's couplets are characterized by their directness, simplicity, and rhythmical tune. He eschewed elaborate metaphors. In an era when Sanskrit and Persian dominated all scholarly knowledge, Kabir pioneered a devotional revolution by using the popular local dialects to convey profound spiritual insights.

Surcharged with wisdom, his compositions have resonated across centuries and cultures with people from all walks of life. As a result, 'Kabir ke Dohe' transcended time and are also a part of school curriculums.

Some of his most esteemed works include *Kabir Bijak*, *Kabir Granthawali*, and *Anurag Sagar*. Though Kabir was illiterate, his literary works and life have become significant subjects of scholarly research. His compositions also hold prominence in the sacred text of Sikhism, the Guru Granth Sahib.

Admonishing Fallacies till His Final Breath

It is believed that Kabir lived for over a hundred years. While he spent most of his life in Kashi, about 200 kilometres away was the city of Maghar. The belief was that leaving one's body in Kashi would merit entry to heaven while dying in Maghar would result in hell.

Kabir wanted to prove the futility of this myth. Saints never miss an opportunity to impart their teachings. When he sensed it was time for him to depart, he left for Maghar. Kabir stated:

*kyā kāśhī kyā ūsar magahar, rām hṛiday bas morā
jo kāsī tan tajai kabīrā, rāme kaun nihorā*

'Be it the holy Kashi or the valley of Maghar, both are the same for me because Ram resides in my heart. If one attains heaven merely by dying in Kashi, then what is the use of devotion to Ram?'

After Kabir's death, a dispute cropped up amongst his Hindu and Muslim followers regarding his last rites. It is said that when the shroud covering his lifeless body was removed, people found only a pile of flowers underneath. These were divided between the Hindus and Muslims. Half of the flowers were taken to Kashi and cremated there, while the other half were buried in Maghar itself.

Like a lotus that blooms in murky waters yet produces immaculate flowers, Kabir was a living symbol of social resurrection amidst turbulent times. With a genuine commitment to reforming society, he tried to establish love and harmony among the people. He equated Ram with Rahim and became a cementing factor between two major conflicting religions. He tried to break people's illusions, not only through the nectar of his poetry but also by practically implementing them in his simple lifestyle. He lived a down-to-earth life but reached sublime heights of wisdom.

He did not care to belong to a particular community, religion, or sect, and instead identified with humanity at large. As an epitome of universal love, Kabir became a legendary and enigmatic figure during his lifetime and beyond.

6

Ravidas

Sant Ravidas, also known as Raidas, was a mystic poet-saint and social reformer in medieval times in North India. He propagated simplicity in devotion to God, free from formal ritualistic practices. The teachings of Ravidas promoted equality, social justice, and compassion for everyone. He became famous for his teachings of universal respect for all, springing from his pure love for the Divine.

Ravidas is also renowned for his hymns, which are imbued with fervent bhakti. Through his compositions, he conveys an array of devotional sentiments. Some bhajans express intense feelings of separation from the Lord, with the deep desire to meet his Beloved. In others, Ravidas emphasizes inner purity over rituals and caste divisions rampant in his time.

Saint Ravidas is also famous as the Guru of Meerabai. Replicas of his lotus feet are installed in the temple of Meerabai in Chittorgarh. She has written of him:

> guru milyo ravidāsajī, dīnī jñān kī guṭakī
> choṭ lagī nijanām harī kī, mhāre hivare khaṭakī

'I found my Guru in Saint Ravidasji, and he bestowed the nectar of divine knowledge. He knocked me down with God's Name;

now Shri Hari's divine name resounds in my heart.'

Birth and Early Years

Sant Ravidas was born to Santokh Das and Kalsi Devi in the sacred city of Varanasi (Kashi), the historical centre for learning and religion. Ravidas' exact date of birth remains ambiguous due to limited records. Scholars believe he was born in 1376–1378 CE.

As per the hagiographies available, Sant Ravidas' story begins with an incident from his previous birth. Swami Ramananda was an eminent saint, preacher, and social reformer in medieval India. He was the Guru of famous saints, such as Kabirdas, Dhanna Jat, and Bhagat Pipa. He resided in an ashram in Kashi along with his *brahmachari* disciples.

One student was responsible for collecting alms from the market. Ramananda forbade him to gather offerings from householders seeking selfish boons in return. He believed that only alms offered selflessly were fit to be offered to his Deity. Consequently, the disciple would discern the intention behind every offering before accepting it. Ramananda would then personally make and offer the bhog to his Deity. He would divinely perceive that the Lord had accepted the food.

Among Kashi's affluent was Raghu Charan, a prosperous but childless leather merchant. Desperate for progeny, he was advised that offering alms to Swami Ramananda might fulfil his wish. However, knowing of his intentions, Ramananda consistently refused his offerings. Undeterred, Raghu Charan devised a plan. He gave grains to a local grocer, along with a sum of money, and requested they be given as alms to Ramananda's disciple.

On a stormy day, cornered by the rain, the disciple took shelter at this very grocer's store. Persuaded by the grocer, and against his better judgement, he accepted the grains and brought them back to the ashram. However, when Swami Ramananda made the offering to his Deity, he felt it was not accepted. This troubled Ramananda immensely. He questioned the disciple, who confessed to accepting Raghu Charan's grains.

Deeply dismayed, Swami Ramananda cursed the disciple to be reborn as a tanner, which was the profession of Raghu Charan. True to the Saint's words, the disciple passed away and was reborn as Raghu's son. The merchant was delighted. He took it as a blessing of Swami Ramananda and became a member of Swamiji's satsang.

The child was named Ravidas. He displayed unusual austerity from infancy, abstaining from all food except his mother's milk. Two years passed, and word of the child's fasting reached Swami Ramananda. Gurudev knew this was his disciple reborn. Concerned, he visited Raghu Charan's home under a pretext. He enquired from the little infant Ravidas as to why he refused to eat. Ravidas recollected the incident from his last life—he had accepted grains from Raghu Charan's home—which had led to the curse. How could he consume such grain now?

Swami Ramananda reassured Ravidas that Raghu Charan and his family were his disciples now. There was no concern about eating their grain. With Ramananda's blessings and assurance, young Ravidas began to eat.

The Generous Heart of Ravidas and Family Strife

As Ravidas grew older, he obtained access to his wealthy father's vault. He had a generous heart and began distributing charity to the needy. While his mother silently approved of his deeds, this secret eventually reached his father, who was aghast. Raghu Charan forbade Ravidas from squandering away the wealth he had so painstakingly earned. In the future, when Ravidas had his own earnings, he could do whatever he wished. However, Ravidas had a deep-seated urge to help and found it impossible to comply with his father's wishes.

In an attempt to make him more responsible, when he was just 14, his parents arranged his wedding. They hoped married life would reduce his generous impulses. Yet, destiny would have it otherwise. Ravidas' wife mirrored his generous spirit and readily supported him. One day, Ravidas' charity exceeded his usual limits, which provoked his father into a fit of rage. Raghu Charan cast Ravidas out of his home.

The irony of the situation is noteworthy. Raghu Charan, who had once fervently beseeched God for a son, was now severing ties with him. Such is the nature of the world. As long as one's desires are fulfilled, relationships seem endearing. However, the moment one does not meet our expectations, our love starts to diminish, and we get detached. This reveals the inherently selfish nature of worldly relationships. Raghu's love for his son was based on self-interest, and when it got harmed, the same Ravidas seemed like an enemy. If Raghu had truly loved his child, he would have been willing to overlook the faults and continue with the relationship.

Expelled from his parent's home, Ravidas and his wife began a new chapter in their life—devoid of comforts and luxuries. Like all of us, Saints too encounter their share of trials and tribulations. In fact, Bhagavan Ram Himself, in His divine pastimes, was exiled to the forest the day He was to be crowned as the King of Ayodhya. Thus, no one is insulated from hardships in this world of maya.

Unlike us, however, the Saints remain undisturbed even in the face of adversity. How are they able to do it? They perceive the grace of God in reversals. They firmly believe that the ultimate purpose of life is the elevation of the soul. So, in challenging conditions, they see the silver lining, which is the opportunity for spiritual growth. It was with this thought that Kunti Devi, mother of the five Pandava brothers, requested hardships from Shree Krishna. The Shreemad Bhagavatam states:

vipadaḥ santu naḥ śhaśhvatatra tatra jagad-guro (1.8.25)

'O Jagadguru Shree Krishna! Please continue to send calamities in my life.' Mother Kunti showed no preference for material comforts. She realized every time she faced a calamity, she felt closer to God internally.

So, from a higher perspective, adversity is not a bad thing. Material luxuries can delude us into believing we can obtain happiness from the world. On the other hand, disappointments open our eyes to the futility of our material pursuits. They serve to catalyse one's detachment. And with detachment, one turns towards God and acquires real wealth, which is divine love, the treasure of the soul. So, let us take inspiration from the Saints. While we may not be elevated enough to ask God for setbacks—as Kunti did—when they come on their own, we should see in them a divine purpose and not get disturbed.

Starting Anew with High Spirits and Renewed Fervour

Ravidas was now on the street and without support. Knowing no other trade than the craft learnt from his father, Ravidas became a cobbler. He would sit in the bustling market square, serving people's footwear needs at fair prices. If anyone questioned his work as demeaning, Ravidas would respond with pride, 'Why should I feel bad? I am privileged to serve the lotus feet of devotees.'

In his menial profession, Ravidas displayed exemplary contentment. This is in sharp contrast to our nature where we always want more, always seeking the next best thing. Social media does an excellent job of making us believe others have it better than us. As the saying goes, 'The grass is always greener on the other side of the fence.' Consequently, people have everything they need, and yet, one possession eludes them—they do not have the thing called 'enough'.

Ravidas, however, was blessed with heaps of 'enough'. Content in his work, he found great joy in service. Such is the feeling among devotees of the Lord—they always harbour the attitude of service in all they do. They regard all work as a means to serve their Beloved Lord. And in doing so, they highlight the importance of humility—considered a crowning virtue on the path of bhakti. This humble perspective, found within many spiritual communities, reflects a profound reverence for menial tasks. For instance, in Gurdwaras, high-ranking officials—from IAS officers to army generals—take pride in performing what seem like lowly tasks, such as attending to shoes.

For Ravidas, his trade was a form of communion with God. Amidst the sounds of the market and the rhythm of his work, he found moments to sing bhajans, infusing his day with devotion. Below is one of his most famed and lovely hymns:

prabhujī tum chandan ham pānī,
 jākī ang ang bāñs samānī
prabhujī tum ghan, ban ham morā,
 jaise chitvat chānd chakorā
prabhujī tum motī ham dhāgā,
 jaise sohane milat suhāgā
prabhujī tum dīpak ham bātī,
 jākī jyotī barai din rātī
prabhujī tum swāmī ham dāsā,
 aisī bhakti karai raidāsā

'O Lord, You are sandalwood, and I am water. Your fragrance fills my entire being, and Your essence pervades everything. O Lord, You are the cloud, and I am Your bird. In the forest of my mind, I look at You as the Chakor bird stares at the moon. O Lord, You are the pearl, and I am Your thread; with You, I feel as if gold has enhanced its splendour. O Lord, You are the lamp, and I am the wick. Your light shines continuously, day and night. O Lord, You are the Master, and I am Your servant. Grant Raidas the blessing of always experiencing such devotion.'

God's Protection and Ravidas' True Philosopher's Stone

Ravidas' life continued in this simple manner. He would mend shoes to meet the bare minimum needs for his family while cheerfully singing devotional bhajans of God. Though times were difficult, he did not care. He had mastered the art of gratitude and saw his life as full of the Lord's infinite blessings.

However, Bhagavan is *bhakta vatsala*—the One who loves His devotees dearly—and He grew uncomfortable with Ravidas's prolonged hardships. The Shreemad Bhagavatam states:

> *aham bhakta-parādhīno hyasvatantra iva dvija* (9.4.63)

Shree Krishna says: 'I am entirely under the control of My devotees and not at all independent.' Such is the amazing relationship between God and the Saints, that the Master of infinite universes becomes enslaved by His devotees' love.

One day, the Lord assumed the guise of a wandering sadhu and approached Ravidas for shoe repairs. His intent was to bestow a small fortune upon him. However, Ravidas politely declined any amount from the sadhu, stating that he did not charge renunciants and serving them was reward enough.

The Lord then gifted a *paras* (philosopher's stone) to Ravidas with which he could alleviate his penurious condition. However, Ravidas declined it as well. For him, the true *paras* was God's Name that transforms sinners into saints and mortals into immortals. Nevertheless, the Lord left the stone with Ravidas hoping he would change his mind and promised to come back after a year. Upon His return, he discovered Ravidas living his simple life and continuing his trade as before.

A while later, Swami Ramananda gave a sacred Shaligram to Ravidas, with the instruction to worship it daily. One day, to Ravidas' astonishment, five gold coins appeared near the Shaligram. Seeing this, Ravidas pointed out the irony of the situation to his wife. The Almighty, who liberates souls, was entangling them in maya—first through the *paras* and now with gold coins!

Ravidas picked up the Shaligram with the intent of immersing it in the Ganges. Seeing this, Lord Narayan Himself appeared before him. The Lord expressed His desire for Ravidas to live in a comfortable home. Ravidas finally accepted it as the Lord's will. Promptly, Narayan inspired a generous donor to arrange for Ravidas' new home. Yet, the new residence made no difference to Ravidas' simple lifestyle. This was akin to the story of Sudama, Shree Krishna's friend, who received a grand palace but preferred to live in it with his tattered clothes.

Moving Beyond Caste and Creed—Ravidas Advocates Equality Through Bhakti

Sant Ravidas was instrumental in propagating social equality in an era marked by severe disparities. Common privileges were denied to those born into a lower caste. They were relegated to inferior living conditions and forced to dwell in huts instead of proper homes at the periphery of villages.

Disturbed by this segregation, Ravidas took it upon himself to elevate the societal position of these oppressed communities. His teachings challenged the prevailing norms, emphasizing that one's actions, rather than birth, define one's character. His poetry explicitly taught universal equality and the importance of good deeds and inner purity. Throughout his life, Ravidas pushed social reform through devotion to God, in which no one was higher or lower. The following incident, taken from hagiographic descriptions of his days in Kashi, illustrates these principles.

After receiving a secure residence, Ravidas settled into his new life in Kashi. He continued with his craft and accumulated some wealth. Having a generous heart, he donated to anyone who would approach him for succour. As a result, his reputation grew as a benefactor and philanthropist. All this while, he continued with his satsang and devotional practices.

Seeing this, the orthodox brahmins of Kashi (the upper caste) became disturbed. Burning with envy, they confronted Ravidas, 'We are brahmins. Why don't you donate to us as well?'

Ravidas openly welcomed their request, inviting them to partake in his generosity. However, the brahmins were not to be pacified. They challenged Ravidas, 'You work with leather. How can you engage in worship of God?'

Ravidas responded calmly, 'If God has no objections, why should you?'

The brahmins were displeased with Ravidas' retort. They petitioned the Hindu king of Kashi. Ravidas was accused of corrupting religious traditions by excluding brahmins from donations, and more grievously, by worshipping the Divine, which was reserved for the upper class.

Ravidas remained undeterred and replied, 'If God accepts my worship, who are they to object?'

The brahmins demanded proof that God accepted his service and proposed a test. A Shaligram was brought. Ravidas was asked to sit on one side, while the brahmins sat on the other. Whichever side the Shaligram chose to move would be declared the winner.

The brahmins began reciting the *Swasti Vachan* and other Vedic mantras, but the Shaligram remained stationary. They intensified their effort without success.

Then came Ravidas' turn. With all humility, he spoke to the Divinity in the Shaligram, 'I am not versed in the scriptures. I know neither the *Swasti Vachan* nor the *Vishnu Sahasranam*. All I can do is sing a few bhajans in service of my Beloved Lord.' With that, he began singing his famous bhajan.

> *aisī lāl tujha binu kaunu karai*
> *garīb nivāju gusāīā merā, māthai chhatru dharai*
> *jākī chhotī jagat kau lāge, tā par tuhīṅ ḍharai*
> *nīchau ūch karai merā gobindū, kāhū te na darai*
> *nāmdev kabīrū tilochanu sadhanā sainu tarai*
> *kahi ravidāsu sunahu re santahu, harijīu te sabhai sarai*

'O Lord! Who else but You could do such a thing? O Support of the destitute! You have put the umbrella of Your Grace over my head. Only You can grant mercy to that person whose touch supposedly pollutes the world. You exalt and elevate the lowly, O my Lord! You are not afraid of anyone. You bestowed salvation to Naamdev, Kabir, Trilochan, Sadana, and Sain. Says Ravidas, "Listen, dear devotees, through the Lord, all is accomplished."'

As he sang, with fervent devotion and childlike faith, the rendering of his bhajan permeated the air. Soon thereafter, the sacred Shaligram gently rolled over and settled in Ravidas' lap. God had pronounced His verdict. The brahmins were crestfallen and bowed their head before Ravidas in reverence.

The king was in awe. Taking this as a God-given sign of Ravidas' divinity, the king became his follower. Subsequently, many other kings and queens too became Ravidas' disciples. This is how he came to be called the *Raj Guru* by his contemporary saints.

Teachings of Ravidas—Purity of Heart Beyond Rituals

Sant Ravidas' path of bhakti was devoid of elaborate rituals. One of his famous sayings was: *mana chañgā to kaṭhautī meṅ gangā* 'If your mind is pure, the holy Ganges resides in your water pot'. This dramatic and pithy statement brilliantly stresses inner purity above and beyond everything else. A touching tale from Ravidas' life elucidates this core spiritual principle.

The king of Kashi had a priest who regularly performed rituals and offerings to Mother Ganges on the king's behalf. This priest would often urge Ravidas to join him for ceremonial dips and poojas. Ravidas would politely decline, with the statement: *mana chañgā to kaṭhautī meṅ gangā* thereby accentuating inner goodness over external acts.

One day, the pandit insisted on taking Ravidas to the Ganges. Instead, Ravidas handed him two bananas and said, 'Offer these to Mother Ganga from my side.'

The brahmin took the bananas to the river, as he was told. However, when he made the offering, a hand emerged from the Ganga to accept it. The priest was shocked by what he saw. Before he could think what to make of it, the hand emerged again. This time, it presented him with a bracelet, saying, 'Give this to Ravidas as a divine gift from Mother Ganga.'

Though he had witnessed an amazing miracle, yet greed clouded the brahmin's judgment. Instead of delivering the bracelet to

Ravidas, he sold it to a goldsmith. From there, it was purchased by a wealthy businessman's wife. Wearing it, she went to meet the queen, who was so enamoured by the bracelet that she purchased it for a hefty price.

Now, the king saw the celestial ornament on his queen's wrist. He was delighted at the bracelet's elegant beauty and thought that there must be another one to complete the pair. He urged the queen to acquire the second bracelet to complement the first.

The king's men traced the bracelet back to the priest and demanded the matching one. The pandit panicked. He realised his deceit would be caught, so he sought Ravidas' help. Being compassionate and soft-hearted, Ravidas agreed to ask Mother Ganga for a second bracelet. Recalling the first incident, the pandit requested two bananas to offer in the river.

Ravidas stated it was not necessary and repeated his aphorism: *mana chañgā to kaṭhautī meṅ gangā*. Sitting in his usual cobbler seat, he took a tumbler of water and prayerfully requested Mother Ganga for a second bracelet. Miraculously, a second bracelet materialized!

This episode deepened the king's reverence for Ravidas, reinforcing the teaching that true love and communion with God are consequences of inner purity. To purify the mind, we must bathe it in devotion to the Supreme. The Ramayan states:

> *milahiṅ na raghupati binu anurāgā,*
> *kieṅ jog tap gyān birāgā*

'Though you may practise yoga and austerities, cultivate bookish knowledge, or display external renunciation, without loving devotion, you will not attain Shree Ram.'

This does not mean that rituals serve no purpose. Most people do need external support to take their mind to the Supreme. Rituals enable them to gradually cultivate devotion in their heart. Besides, religious procedures facilitate the continuity of culture. They can conveniently be passed from one generation to the next. In contrast, inner devotion is a very subtle science. Teaching it to children becomes a challenge unless it is accompanied by physical practices.

Thus, rituals per se should be derided. They tie society to the external adherence of dharma. As the adage goes, 'something is better than nothing'. Likewise, injunctions for Vedic ceremonial practices prevent people from becoming frivolous.

That said, once people develop a certain level of bhakti, the importance of religious procedures diminishes. Their mind is now naturally engaged in loving devotion, which was the goal of all rituals. At this stage, rituals become counterproductive when people remain stuck in them, ignoring their ultimate purpose. They visit holy sites but carry worldly thoughts within. They adorn deities externally but neglect inner purity. They bathe in sacred rivers yet harbour ignoble thoughts. Consequently, their mind remains impure.

Thus, the very scriptures that prescribed rituals in the first place, also condemn them for sincere sadhaks. They repeatedly remind us that without cultivating beautiful and noble sentiments, Vedic ceremonies are merely empty physical drills.

The Shreemad Bhagavatam states the true essence of rituals is to know and attain God:

> vāsudeva-parā vedā vāsudeva-parā makhāḥ
> vāsudeva-parā yogā vāsudeva-parāḥ kriyāḥ
> vāsudeva-param jñānaṁ vāsudeva-param tapaḥ
> vāsudeva-paro dharmo vāsudeva-parā gatiḥ (1.2.28–29)

'The Supreme Divine Personality, Shree Krishna, is the ultimate object of knowledge. The goal of all Vedic sacrifices is to please Him. The purpose of yogic practice is to realize Him. Every ritual is meant for Shree Krishna's pleasure. He is the Ultimate Truth, and all severe austerities should aim at knowing Him. Dharma involves offering loving service to Him. He is the supreme goal of your life.'

Last Days and Legacy

Ravidas lived a long life in Kashi, and there were many famous incidents to his name. Each one had associated learnings—love for God, humility, equality, transient nature of the world, and inner purity. Details of his death, including date and cause, remain elusive. Historical texts present ambiguous narratives suggesting death due to natural causes. However, this is a moot point because Ravidas' legacy continues in his numerous compositions and literature. His works are preserved in the Guru Granth Sahib (holy scripture of the Sikhs), which contains 40 of his *padas* (verses), as well as in the *Pancha Vani* and other collections.

The profound teachings of Sant Ravidas became the basis for the *Ravidassia* faith, a sect that regards him as their Supreme Guru. In India and the world over, this community continues to celebrate his principles and practices. Sant Ravidas Jayanti, birth anniversary of the Saint, is also jubilantly celebrated all over India, especially in Varanasi. Its observance has ensured the preservation of Ravidas' devotional music and serves as a forum for discussing topics related to equality and social justice. There are also many temples and memorials that commemorate his life. Thus, even today, seekers continue to find inspiration and spiritual guidance in Sant Ravidas' literature, festivals, and holy places connected to him.

7

Andal

Andal was an icon of prodigious devotion. She was the only woman among the 12 Alvar poet-saints of the Shri Vaishnav tradition. The word *Alvar* signifies 'one who is immersed in the experience of God'. They were the pioneers and propagators of the Bhakti Movement in South India.

The Alvars were profoundly devoted to Bhagavan Vishnu. They designated 108 temples of Bhagavan Vishnu in Bharat as *Divya Desams*, meaning 'Divine Abodes'. This immensely popularized the worship of Lord Vishnu (Narayan) and His various avatars.

By the fifth century, South India was embroiled in fierce religious conflicts. The prevailing Buddhist and Jain ideas were getting displaced by the devotional path propagated by the Nayanars (Shaivite bhakti saints). Eventually, all other philosophies were ousted from royal patronage too.

In this turbulent era, the Nayanars and Alvars championed the path of pure devotion. It was a revolutionary form of worship presenting the Divine as *saulabhyam*, or 'easily accessible to all'. Keeping this in mind, they composed prayers and hymns in their mother tongue to foster a direct connection with the

Divine. This movement led to the reconversion of kings to Hinduism and to object to the caste system of medieval Indian society.

Andal was known by many names, such as Kodai, Nachiyar, Godai, and Goda Devi. She saw Narayan as her Divine Beloved. This manifested in her desire to be the bride of Lord Ranganathaswamy in Srirangam, not just in her mind and spirit but also as a living maiden. Immersed in devotional ecstasy, she offered fervent songs of worship to God.

Andal embodied *madhurya bhav* (conjugal sentiments for God) reminiscent of the gopis' love for Shree Krishna. Her verses amply depict selfless devotion and ultimate surrender to God. Andal's poetic expressions of longing for Bhagavan Narayan were unique and transcended conventional worship. She not only glorified Vishnu in His various avatars but also intimately chides Him in profound yearning.

Andal perfectly encapsulated *viraha bhav*, or love in separation. Her adoration of Narayan was in a class of its own, as she saw her Divine Beloved everywhere in the world surrounding her. Eventually, Andal entered the sacred precincts of the Ranganathaswamy Temple. There, she married the magnificent deity, the resplendently bejewelled Lord slumbering on the coils of the serpent Anant Shesh. The holy ceremony was conducted with the Utsav Murti of the Lord.

Andal's songs, expressing the finest devotional sentiments to the Lord, contributed greatly to promoting the path of bhakti in South India for many centuries. In the sixteenth century, the great king of Vijayanagar, Maharaj Krishnadevaraya, composed an epic poem titled *Āmuktamālyada*. In 875 verses and prose passages, he narrated the life of Goda Devi.

Indeed, Godai's lovelorn compositions, a testament to her profound devotion, continue to be venerated and recited in the thousand-pillared hall of the Ranganathaswamy Temple to this day.

Discovery of an Alvar by an Alvar

Andal appeared in Srivilliputhur, a temple town in Tamil Nadu located close to the Western Ghats. Historians believe she was born during the ninth century, in the Tamil month of Adi. She appeared as a beautiful baby under a tulsi plant in the garden of the Vatapatrasayi temple, where Periyalvar would serve the Lord.

Godai was discovered by the renowned Alvar, Periyalvar, famously known as Vishnuchitta. He lovingly took the infant to the Lord's feet and beseeched Him to accept her. Narayan instructed Periyalvar to look after the baby as his own daughter and to name her *Kodai*, meaning 'a beautiful garland of flowers'. Paying obeisance to the Lord, he brought the baby home to his pious wife, who rejoiced on becoming a mother.

In his personal devotion, Periyalvar was driven by *vatsalya bhav* (parental love) towards Narayan. He cared for the Lord's well-being and blessed Him. In his endearing hymns, he cherishes hugging Krishna as his own son. It is said that God reciprocates with a devotee in the way he surrenders to Him. No wonder Periyalvar had the opportunity to serve Andal as his own child.

On Kodai, he showered deep affection and care, befitting a parent. He was the first to acknowledge her unique bond with the Lord. Eventually, he escorted his daughter to the temple to unite her with her Divine Beloved and returned home alone.

The Precocious Child

Kodai was remarkable even as an infant, babbling only the name of Bhagavan Narayan. Unlike other girls of her age, she disdained playing with childish dolls. Instead, she loved hearing the enchanting tales of Shree Krishna.

One day, little Kodai darted into the house from the garden and hid behind her father's legs. Periyalvar lovingly asked her what she was up to. 'I am hiding from Krishna. Don't tell Him!' came the innocent and playful response. Periyalvar realized his daughter perceived Krishna more profoundly than he did.

As Kodai started growing, her heart brimmed with love for Bhagavan Vishnu. She began to spend all her time in devotion. Like her father, she gathered flowers. She assisted him in weaving garlands for the deity at the local temple. Other times, she would sing songs full of devotional love to please the Lord.

Once, Kodai was playing a game with her friends. They suggested she draw circles in the sand with her fingers while blindfolded. Only if the ends of her circles met would it be a sure sign that Krishna would marry her. And thus came an earnest prayer from young Kodai's heart, 'If the Lord who danced on the Kaaliya Serpent is going to marry me, then let the circle ends meet.' Miraculously, each time she attempted, they did.

Kodai's innocent love transformed Srivilliputhur into Vrindavan, where Krishna's presence and Leelas were tangible. Young Kodai assumed the role of a gopi, serving Krishna with utmost love, along with her friends. She considered them her fellow cowherd maidens, calling them all to worship Krishna together. Lord Ranganathan in the local temple became Shree Krishna, while she was His gopi.

Along with her playmates, young Kodai reenacted scenes from Shree Krishna's life, creating a world filled with divine play. She would fashion an earthen hut, and then imagine Krishna, in His mischievousness, dismantling it. She would be bathing in the Yamuna along with other gopis, and Krishna would hide their clothes.

In a beautiful composition, she exhorts her friends to join her in worshipping Krishna. Let us savour the flavours of Andal's devotion through this translation:

'Awaken, O beloved ones of sweet Vrindavan! The birds are singing melodiously, and the sound of the temple conch echoes in the atmosphere. Can you not hear the call? Can you not hear the churning of the yoghurt by the gopis? Are your ears impaired for these sacred sounds? Let us bathe in the shimmering waters of Yamuna and sing the glories of Krishna, the Flute-bearer of Vrindavan, the joy of Yashoda, and offer Him fresh flowers in worship.

'Rise, O daughters! Do not linger in slumber. Arise quickly, for the Brahma Muhurt is slipping away. At this auspicious hour, let us praise the One who killed all the demons, the One who lies on the bed of *Anant Shesh* in the ocean of milk, the One who is the Seed of the universe.'

Through the wake-up call to her friends, Kodai actually prodded all souls under maya to awaken from the deep slumber of ignorance and bathe in the divine love of Shree Krishna. Just as one cools the body by diving into a pond, so does the soul find eternal peace by diving into the ocean of devotion.

Later in life, Andal composed exquisite poems describing the Lord's delightfully sweet and charming Pastimes.

Kodai and her friends would also enact the marriage of Lakshmi and Narayan with dolls, singing wedding songs extolling the Lord's virtues. Listening to these songs over and over again, Kodai would fall into a trance. Seeing the Lord in every particle, she transcended physical existence. Though she physically resided in the house of Periyalvar, her spirit was in Vrindavan with the gopis and Shree Krishna. As she entered adolescence, she began to see Krishna not as a Playmate but as her Lover.

Offering of Worn Garland to the Lord

Being the daughter of the temple's garland maker, young Kodai would lovingly weave a garland and then hand it to her father to offer to the deity. In her boundless love and innocence, she would first wear the garland herself.

Gazing into the mirror, she would say, 'O Lord Ranganatha! My Darling Beloved! Do You love my beauty now?' She pondered whether her beauty was worth offering to her Beloved Lord Vishnu, whom she worshipped as her Husband. Periyalvar was unaware of his daughter's private moments of devotion to the Lord.

One day, the temple priest discovered a strand of hair in the garland brought by Periyalvar. The priest refused to accept it, so Periyalvar had to weave a fresh garland as part of his daily service. On another occasion, the priest complained that the garland looked wilted.

Periyalvar trusted his daughter completely and could not understand why the garlands did not look fresh. To uncover the truth, he decided to secretly observe the activities in his house. Hiding behind a curtain, he watched Kodai joyously wear the fresh garland and speak to Bhagavan Vishnu in the mirror.

Now Periyalvar was furious. He rebuked his daughter for defiling the Lord's garland. She had rendered it unfit for the Deity by first wearing it herself. He warned her never to repeat such a mistake. Then, making a fresh garland, he gave it to the priest at the temple.

That night, Bhagavan Vishnu appeared in Periyalvar's dream and addressed him as 'father-in-law'. He said, 'The garlands worn by Andal are most pleasing to Me. She is My bride. Bring Me only the garlands that she has worn.'

Periyalvar realized Kodai's genuine devotion for the Lord and the Almighty's acceptance of her. From that day, Kodai came to be known as *Chudi Koduththa Nachiyar,* meaning 'one who tried the garlands on herself before giving them to God'.

This episode reminds us of Shabari, who offered her half-eaten berries to Bhagavan Ram in her humble hut. Despite belonging to the royal Kshatriya lineage, Shree Ram accepted the berries and delightfully relished them.

Similarly, Shree Krishna, as the king of Dwarka, looked forward to eating the dry rice from His impoverished friend, Sudama. He even savoured the banana peels that Vidurani offered Him, overwhelmed by her love.

How wondrous that the Supreme Master of the entire creation—whose mere thought creates and dissolves multitudes of universes—cherishes even the humblest offerings given with genuine love. While the world pays importance to externals, God notes our inner thoughts.

This was precisely the case with Kodai as well. Though it seemed she was offering a used and impure garland, in reality, it was an exquisite tapestry of devotion for her Divine Beloved. Her whole being was love personified. No wonder Narayan was endeared to accept her as His consort.

Yearning in Youth

When Kodai came of age, Periyalvar began searching for a suitable bridegroom within his community. However, Kodai resolutely told her father that she would not marry any mortal. Her mind was centred on Lord Ranganatha, and she had dedicated her life to Him alone.

Kodai's mother reproached Periyalvar for being lax and allowing her freedom with her devotional thoughts. As a father, Periyalvar, too, had concerns. But he knew that when the Divine enters the heart, all rules dissolve. His daughter had chosen her path unaware of regulations and without care for them.

There was not even a single moment that Andal did not think of her Beloved. Every aspect of her daily routine—bathing, dressing, cooking, and singing—revolved around her Lord. King Krishnadevaraya has beautifully captured Andal's myriad emotions in his poetic masterpiece, *The Āmuktamālyada*. Let us savour the translation of some verses:

'O friends! The songs you sing of Vishnu's might,
Seem unjust and far from right.
For all the women who gave Him their heart,
He left them without a second thought.'   (verse 40)

'That Vishnu does pastimes of a God, a Sage, or a King,
Stirring millions of hearts that to Him would cling,
It would have been better if He'd stayed the same,
As a fish, a turtle, a boar with no such love game!' (verse 41)

'For in those forms, He had no bride,
For an animal's love isn't deep and tried,

Love is an emotion an animal cannot confide,
They can't feel the yearning that we humans do,
Don't you see? I know this to be true.'   (verse 42)

Andal's friends could not understand her genuine love for Bhagavan Vishnu. Beneath her playful taunts, her words unveiled her true feelings. Externally, her body glowed like molten gold in the intense pain of separation from her Beloved.

In the next verses of *The Āmuktamālyada*, Kodai's friends reveal her earlier incarnation as Satyabhama, followed by her own affirmative response:

'O Goda! Wasn't it you, who felt jealousy rise,
When you saw Rukmini with the heavenly flower as a prize?
With envy and spite, you caused such a fret,
For a single flower would not have your heart set,
A tiny ask became a grand quest,
When you made Him fetch the whole tree at your behest!
O Goda, are you not the same Satyabhama?'   (verse 74)

'There was once, when Krishna had kept me in His heart's fane.
But now in this Kaliyuga, I have come again.
To suffer the agony of separation
Why must I bear this corporeal deterioration?
Before my father gives me to another's embrace,
I'll end my life and reach my Lord's grace!'   (verse 80)

As her longing for the Lord intensified, Andal's physical health began to decline. She lost weight, neglected even the basic ornamentation rituals that women of her time followed religiously, and forsook sleep and food.

While Periyalvar empathized with his daughter's lovelorn state, the people of the town complained about Kodai's visibly deteriorating health. They felt she was inflicted with a mental disease and needed to get married to be cured. When Andal heard these kinds of talks, she exclaimed: 'Yes! I am captured by a black figure, but it is not a devil possessing me. It is none other than my Divine, dark-hued Lord, Shree Krishna, Who has seized my heart and my soul. Only He shall be my Beloved. If I am forced to be with another man, I would rather give up my life than betray this sacred bond.'

Once, Kodai asked her father about sacred pilgrimages. Periyalvar described various holy places, including Lord Ranganathaswamy's abode in Srirangam. Thrilled on hearing this, tears welled up in Kodai's eyes. On further prodding, Periyalvar narrated the tale of Prabhu Ram and His loyal servant Vibheeshan.

After conquering Lanka, Lord Ram returned to Ayodhya with an entourage, including Vibheeshan. When Vibheeshan was asked to return to Lanka to rule, he could not bear the separation from Shree Ram. He requested a souvenir that would appease his heart. Lord Ram then gave him the deity of Shri Ranganathaswamy, instructing him not to keep it down before reaching Lanka. However, during his aerial travel from Ayodhya to Lanka, the deity grew heavier and heavier, and the exhausted Vibheeshan placed the deity in Srirangam in Tamil Nadu.

Lord Ranganathaswamy thereafter refused to accompany Vibheeshan to Lanka. Vibheeshan, therefore, built a temple of the Lord there and visited daily from Lanka.

Hearing these divine pastimes, Andal's attraction towards Lord Ranganathaswamy deepened. Her devotion grew so intense that she could no longer bear separation from Him, even for a moment. With persistent tears in anguish, she pleaded her Beloved to accept her at His feet. Kodai's love for the Lord was ablaze with fervent and profound passion. She longed for Him akin to a woman pining for union with her lover by way of marriage. Such *viraha bhav* for the Supreme has been greatly extolled in the Vedic scriptures and by great Saints.

The Divine Intervention and Marriage to Lord Ranganatha

Lord Ranganatha fulfilled Kodai's deepest desire by marrying her.

One day, He appeared in the dreams of the priests in Srirangam. He told them to bring His beloved Andal immediately and facilitate a grand wedding. They were instructed to bring Andal in the same palanquin that was used for the Lord Himself and perform the same worship rituals which were offered to Him.

Simultaneously, the Lord appeared in Periyalvar's dream, requesting him to adorn Kodai as a bride. The same night, Andal saw in her dream that she was being married to the Lord with great ostentation and fanfare.

The next morning, the house was decorated with coconuts, mango leaves, and sandalwood paste, ready for a beautiful wedding. Festive music played in the background, and Kodai was dressed as a bride. As instructed, priests from Srirangam arrived at the house of Periyalvar. They were ready to escort the Lord's bride in the palanquin to the Ranganathaswamy Temple. The air was filled with the resounding echoes of conches, the uproar of musical instruments, and the palpable ecstasy of the crowd. Kodai was escorted with unparalleled grandeur to Srirangam. The procession included Periyalvar, his friends and family, along with the royal family of Madurai and its entourage.

Kodai, the embodiment of devotion, was welcomed in the temple amidst the chanting of Vedic mantras. The wedding of Kodai and Lord Ranganatha was performed outside the sanctum sanctorum in the Srirangam temple, following all traditional marriage rituals. After the ceremony, the Deity was placed back in the sanctum, and Kodai, in the presence of all, merged into the lotus feet of Lord Ranganathaswamy forever.

A divine light engulfed the temple as the lover and her Beloved united. Lord Ranganatha and Kodai became One. This event, known as the *Kodai Kalyanam*, represents the highest expression of devotion. Kodai then became known as *Andal*, meaning 'One Who Rules the Lord'. Since she obtained the grace and love of Lord Ranganatha, Kodai was also named *Ranganayaki*.

In the Bhagavad Gita, Shree Krishna entreats Arjun to unite his consciousness with God in Yog. Andal practised these teachings in their true spirit by dedicating all her thoughts and actions to the Almighty. Such a complete communion with the Lord through bhakti yog resulted in her oneness with the Supreme. It was a testament to the transformative power of devotion.

Enchanting Compositions

As a bhakti saint, Andal composed her hymns in *Cen* or Old Tamil. Her first work, *Tiruppavai* (The Path to Krishna), was composed when she was about thirteen. It is a lyrical description of the vows undertaken by young women to obtain a good husband. Andal composed this during the Margsheesh fasting month (November–December), inspired by a Leela narrated in the Shreemad Bhagavatam.

Tiruppavai states how the gopis performed a fast in honour of Katyayani Devi to attain Shree Krishna as their husband. So, Andal also fasted like the gopis, but when the Lord did not appear at the end of her fast, she felt dejected thinking that her bhakti had not been accepted by the Lord. That is when Andal delivered her yearnings for the Lord in *Nachiyar Tirumozhi* (The Sacred Songs of the Lady).

Nachiyar Tirumozhi is an expression of Andal's *madhurya bhav*. It depicts the longing for both physical and spiritual union with her Beloved. In her devotional intensity and anguish, she scolds and even rages against Him while demanding His embrace. Bhagavan Vishnu is known as *Hari*, meaning 'who takes away sorrow'. Therefore, Andal repeatedly beseeches Hari to accept her and relieve her of suffering.

The *Nachiyar Tirumozhi* has 14 hymns. The sixth song, *Varanam Aayiram*, is prominently used even today. This is a wedding hymn in which Andal envisions herself as the bride and the Lord of the universe as her groom. The hymn's auspicious nature makes it a part of every Tamil Vaishnav marriage ceremony.

In her compositions, Andal addresses the Lord by His various names: as Narayan (who rests on the serpent *Anant Shesh*), as Narayan Nampi (Universal Abode), Tirumal or Mal (The Dark One of Tamil theology), and other prominent Avatars, such as Shree Ram, Vaman Avatar, Bhagavan Narsingh, and more. But most often, she addresses Him as Krishna, her Divine Lover.

Andal's understanding of the Lord is shown in her poetic talent. Her *Tiruppavai* composition begins with the word *Margazhi*, synonymous with Shree Krishna. The Lord Himself states this in the Bhagavad Gita:

māsānāṁ mārga-śhīrṣho 'ham ṛitūnāṁ kusumākaraḥ

(verse 10.35)

'Of the twelve months of the Hindu calendar, I am Margsheersh, and of seasons, I am spring, which brings forth flowers.'

The *Tiruppavai* and the *Nachiyar Tirumozhi* are included in the eleventh century compilation of *Nalayira Divya Prabandham* (four thousand divine hymns) by Nammalvar. This text is highly revered by Shri Vaishnavas and is respected as the *Tamil Veda*. It is used in temples for incantation during ritualistic ceremonies.

In this way, the cultural legacy of Andal's compositions continues to vibrate in South India today.

Jagadguru Ramanujacharya, who descended 400 years after Andal, was her ardent devotee. Renowned as the proponent of *Vishishta Advaita vada,* Ramanujacharya is credited for synthesizing the Vaishnavism of the Alvars with Vedic philosophy. He used to recite Andal's compositions with great religious fervour.

Inspirations

Andal was born at a time when girls were married and had children by their teenage years. Defying the mores of her time, she refused marriage to a mortal man, causing incessant wagging of many tongues in the town. But Andal was unfazed by the ways of the society. Her devotion was as natural and inevitable as the blooming of a flower. With profound and sacred thoughts, she transformed her small temple town into Krishna's divine dwelling.

Andal's heart composed poems throughout the year. Her persistent state of intense melancholy is captured in the *Karkotal Pukkal* (Dark Flowers) composition. In it, she laments that blossoms have burst into beauty and then faded away, the rainy season has also come and gone, yet Andal remains waiting for her Beloved. She clings to the assurances given by the Lord to other devotees, hoping she will not be forsaken.

Andal believed that everything in creation, both material and spiritual, emanates from Him. Each of her *pasurams* (hymns) is imbued with her perception of the Sacred in all life and eloquently conveys her exclusive surrender to the Lord. Just as the ocean is the source of clouds and rain, the Lord is the eternal source of all things. He illuminates the three worlds. Hence, everything that is manifest and unmanifest in the universe is the glory of Bhagavan.

Andal's life has inspired generations for millennia. The *madhurya bhav* bhakti that Andal espoused became a trend in her time. God became the cherished husband of innumerable devotionally-minded women. Kulasekhara Alvar dedicated his daughter, Cherakula Valli Nachiyar, to Lord Ranganathaswamy. Many others followed.

Even today, people participate in multifarious opportunities to serve the Lord's eternal consort, Andal, in the Ranganathaswamy Temple. Each dawn, the first puja is conducted in the Andal shrine. The garland worn by her bejewelled deity through the night is then ceremoniously carried to the shrine of the reclining God. The slightly wilted garland is draped around His neck, symbolizing her fearless love. By afternoon, the garland is gifted to the deity of Periyalvar in his shrine nearby.

Andal's poetic renderings have found merit in literature, rituals, theatre, cinema, dance, painting, and other art forms, perpetuating her influence till date. Thus, her work has permeated modern Indian traditions and heritage. Such accessibility has demystified the bhakti experience, inspiring artists, poets, philosophers, and scholars alike.

Samadhi

Andal, the youngest and only female Alvar saint to be deified, holds a unique place in spiritual history.

Born of Mother Earth, she is also called *Godai*, meaning 'daughter of the Earth' because etymologically, *go* means 'earth' and *da* means 'given by'. Some refer to her as *Goda Devi*, or 'an incarnation of Bhoomi Devi (Mother Earth), one of the three eternal consorts of Lord Vishnu'.

Answering Periyalvar's prayers, the Lord resides with His eternal consort, Andal, as deities in a temple in Srivilliputhur. Constructed on the very site where Kodai lived with her father, this temple is one of the 108 *Divya Desams*.

People engage in elaborate worship of Andal and her Lord here. All the honours accorded to the Lord are also fully extended to Andal. Every year, Their wedding anniversary is celebrated with great splendour in the temples of South India, commemorating Their divine union.

8

Ramanujacharya

Ramanujacharya is venerated as a profound Vedic philosopher and social reformer, who lived during the eleventh and twelfth centuries in southern India. He is renowned as the foremost proponent of *Vishishta Advaita* philosophy, also known as Qualified Non-Dualism. His teachings had a profound impact across the region, significantly contributing to preserving and promoting the devotional hymns of the Alvars.

Ramanujacharya was nurtured in the Shri Vaishnav tradition, which worships Bhagavan Vishnu as the Supreme Deity. He traversed the entire country on foot to revive and fortify Sanatan Dharma. During his lifetime and travels, he emerged as a crusader for social justice and equality. Ramanuja's bold stance on social evils gathered him a lot of enemies, but he overcame all the opposition with his compassion and penance. His contributions to the downtrodden sections and oppressed classes of society were remarkable. Perceived by many as a giant amongst Saints, he continues to be worshipped in several South Indian temples even today.

Before delving into the life of Jagadguru Ramanujacharya and his teachings, it would be beneficial to know about the Shri Vaishnav tradition and its lineage. The Vedas are an ocean of knowledge for all kinds of seekers. They have three sections dealing with karma, jnana, and bhakti. The Shri Vaishnav philosophy emphasizes performing rituals with a devout mindset as offerings to the Lord. In doing so, it beautifully harmonizes all three sections of the Vedas.

Shri Vaishnav Tradition

Nearly two thousand years ago, Shankaracharya propagated *Advaita Vedanta* philosophy across India, which focused heavily on scholarly knowledge. Simultaneously, the Alvars championed the Bhakti Movement in South India, focusing purely on devotion. They popularized the worship of Bhagavan Vishnu in many temples.

Nathamuni was a great Vaishnav Acharya who came after the Alvars. He made Srirangam his headquarters to advance the Bhakti Movement. He compiled the *Tamil Veda*, drawing from the compositions of the Alvars. It contains 4000 *prabandhams* (poems), which are sung even today in South Indian temples as a part of worship ceremonies.

Nathamuni groomed his grandson, Yamunacharya, to preserve and spread the rich Shri Vaishnav heritage. Yamunacharya wrote many compositions in Sanskrit, as a consequence of which he won the respect of scholars. Yamunacharya settled in Srirangam to propagate Shri Vaishnavism. Knowing his days were numbered, he sought a successor who could emancipate society—spiritually, socially, and culturally.

Nathamuni had predicted the birth of a great devotee who would propound the Shri Vaishnav school of thought. When the time came, Yamunacharya identified the young Ramanujacharya as his successor, who went on to become the most influential philosopher of *Vishishta Advaita*.

The Child of a Prophecy

Ramanujacharya was born into a devout Brahmin family in Sriperumbudur, about 40 kilometres from present-day Chennai. His mother, Kantimati, and father, Keshav, Somayaji, were ardent devotees of Bhagavan Vishnu. They performed a yajna to beget a son. Upon the birth of their son, Kantimati's brother, Shailapurna, also known as Nambi, visited the newborn. He could foresee divine qualities in the infant. It dawned upon him that Nammalvar's prediction that a great acharya would be born to propagate the Shri Vaishnav school of thought had been fulfilled.

Nambi named his nephew *Ramanuja*, meaning 'Ram's anuj (younger brother)', *Lakshman*. Throughout his life, Ramanujacharya was revered by both names, Ramanuja and Lakshman. He has also been referred to as *Ilaya Perumal*, meaning 'the radiant one'.

Guided by his erudite father, Ramanuja immersed himself in the study of numerous scriptures in Sriperumbudur. He was frequently visited by Kanchipurna, a renowned disciple of Yamunacharya, from the pilgrimage site of Kanchipuram. Despite belonging to a low caste, Kanchipurna's profound devotion to God greatly influenced Ramanuja's formative years.

Ramanuja was married at the age of 16. Unfortunately, his father died soon after. This loss left Ramanuja disenchanted, and he decided to relocate with his family to Kanchipuram to have a lasting association with his spiritual mentor, Kanchipurna.

Under the Umbrella of an Advaiti Guru

In Kanchipuram, Ramanuja enrolled in the school of Yadav Prakash, an esteemed *Advaiti* guru. Gurudev would emphatically teach the non-dualistic philosophy: *jīvo brahmaiva nā paraḥ* 'There is no separate God beyond the soul'.

Hearing his guru deny the paramount position of the Supreme Divinity troubled Ramanuja deeply. At times, when he tried to voice alternative views, Yadav Prakash would not hide his displeasure and would chastise him severely. Once, after school hours, Ramanuja was serving Yadav Prakash by massaging his feet. Another disciple sought the meaning of a mantra from the *Chhandogya Upanishad*:

tasya yathā kapyāsam puṇḍarīkamevamakṣhiṇī (1.6.7)

This verse describes the beauty of the Lord's eyes. However, Yadav Prakash did not believe that God has a Form. Misinterpreting it, he said: 'This verse likens the redness of the Lord's eyes to the rear-end of a monkey.' One meaning of the word *kapi* in Sanskrit is 'monkey'.

Hearing such humiliating words for the Supreme, boiling hot tears rolled out of Ramanuja's eyes and fell on his guru's feet. This caught the guru's attention, and he inquired about the reason for them. Ramanuja candidly expressed his pain on hearing such profanity for his Beloved Lord. Yadav Prakash then challenged Ramanuja for a better explanation.

Ramanuja explained that *puṇḍarīka* means 'lotus', while

kapyāsam means 'blossomed by the sun'. The mantra thus compares the Lord's eyes to a lotus blossomed by the sun.

Such an exquisite explanation wounded Yadav Prakash's ego. He reprimanded Ramanuja for boasting superiority over his guru and disrespecting the lineage of Adi Shankaracharya. From that day on, tension simmered in the gurukul between Ramanuja and Yadav Prakash.

The situation climaxed when both were summoned to solve a problem for the king. His daughter was possessed by a ghost, and the king wanted it exorcized. Initially, the famed Yadav Prakash was called to drive out the ghost. When Yadav Prakash approached the ghost, it mocked him and demanded he call his disciple, Ramanuja. Upon Ramanuja's arrival, the unusual spirit requested his foot dust as a blessing. When the demand was met, the ghost departed from the princess.

Ramanuja's mere presence had exorcized the ghost, highlighting his profound spiritual power. This incident further shattered Yadav Prakash's pride. He realized that eventually Ramanuja's presence would engender the shutdown of his gurukul.

Saved from an Assassination Attempt

Yadav Prakash viewed Ramanuja as a threat to his hard-earned reputation. To eliminate this perceived danger, Yadav Prakash conspired with his coterie of disciples who were only interested in obtaining a graduation certificate from a prominent guru. Hence, with a servile attitude, they complied with their guru's evil scheme.

Shortly thereafter, Yadav Prakash declared that the class would go on a pilgrimage to the Holy Ganga in the north to wash away their sins. In those days, the only means of travel was on foot so the journey would take a few months. Along the way, the group would have to walk through highlands and lowlands, dangerous forests and peaceful villages, cross gushing rivers and gentle streams, and face violent animals and poisonous reptiles. In such circumstances, Yadav Prakash was sure that they would be able to find an opportunity to kill Ramanuja, which could easily be attributed to an accident due to the dangerous conditions.

The kind-hearted and gentle Ramanuja was eager to undertake the journey with this teacher to the Holy Ganga. He had no inclination of the true reason or the calamity that would befall him. As usual, his cousin Govind, who was like his shadow, would go along as well.

En route in the jungle, Yadav Prakash chose a spot to rest and sent Ramanuja to fetch some water. Seizing the moment, Yadav Prakash instructed his disciples to kill him in the dense forest. Govind overheard this sinister plot and ran to Ramanuja to warn him. On hearing this, Ramanuja fled while Govind returned to the guru.

When Ramanuja did not return by nightfall, Yadav Prakash and the disciples assumed he had fallen prey to some wild animals. While internally jubilant, outwardly, they shed crocodile tears and feigned mourning. Yadav Prakash philosophized on the immortality of the soul to console Govind. After a few hours, the troupe began the journey back to Kanchipuram.

Meanwhile, Ramanuja was disoriented and lost in the treacherous jungle. The 18-year-old was terrified of spending the night alone in a dense forest. However, reminding himself that Bhagavan Narayan was his true Protector, Ramanuja calmed his anxious heart by meditating on the Lord. Gradually, he became fearless.

Unexpectedly, Ramanuja encountered a hunter couple in the forest. Learning of his desire to reach Kanchipuram, they suggested he could join them as they were also on their way to visit the Lord Varadaraja Swamy Temple. Ramanuja appreciated the couple's gesture and accepted their invitation.

At night, they decided to rest at a place. The wife was thirsty, but her husband advised her to go to sleep with the assurance he would fetch her water in the morning. Wanting to help, Ramanuja rose at dawn to search for river water. Upon his return, he found the couple had vanished. Puzzled and saddened, Ramanuja now wondered how to reach Kanchipuram. Just then, he saw a temple on the horizon, towering over the trees. A passerby recognized him as the bright student, Ramanuja, and informed him that he was already in Kanchipuram.

Ramanuja suddenly had a revelation that Bhagavan Narayan and Mother Lakshmi had come in disguise and personally guided him to his destination. Overwhelmed with gratitude, he shed tears and made his way home, where his family rejoiced at his return. Weeks later, when Yadav Prakash returned to the gurukul with the rest of his students, he was utterly shocked to see Ramanuja alive in Kanchipuram. He claimed to have searched for him everywhere and was overjoyed to find him safe.

Despite knowing his guru's reality, Ramanuja went back to

the gurukul. This incident elucidates the magnanimity of Ramanuja's heart. Although aware of his guru's murderous intentions, he harboured no bitterness. He had mastered the virtues of forgiveness, empathy, and patience.

Sought by the Head of Shri Vaishnav Sampradaya

When Yamunacharya, the venerable leader of the Shri Vaishnav Sampradaya, was around a hundred years old, he worried about finding the next Acharya to propagate the mission. Residing in Srirangam, his headquarters, he frequently pondered over this matter. Once, he visited Kanchipuram to have darshan of Lord Varadaraja Swamy. During this visit, he could not help but notice the young and radiant Ramanuja standing next to Yadav Prakash.

Yamunacharya had already heard about this brilliant young man. Years ago, the young Ramanuja had written a commentary on a particular verse, establishing devotional service to God as the highest goal of life. It was in stark contrast to the *Advaita* philosophy, which marginalized the importance of bhakti and regarded the soul itself as God. Ramanuja's logical and convincing explanation had spread far and even reached Yamunacharya. Upon reading it, he recognized it as divinely inspired. Since then, the great head of the Shri Vaishnavas, Yamunacharya, had long desired to meet Ramanuja.

Now in Kanchipuram, seeing Ramanuja for the first time, Yamunacharya was dismayed to find him with Yadav Prakash, an *Advaiti* guru. Visiting the temple, Yamunacharya offered heartfelt prayers to Lord Varadaraja Swamy to have Ramanuja as his disciple.

Quitting Gurukul

Tensions between Ramanuja and his guru steadily escalated within the gurukul. Ramanuja often interrupted Yadav Prakash during the latter's distorted interpretations of Vedic mantras. The breaking point occurred over a debate on these mantras:

sarvam khalvidam brahma, neha nānāsti kiñchana
(*Nirlamba Upanishad*, verse 9)

sarvam khalvidam brahma, tajjalāniti śhānta upāsīta
(*Chhandogya Upanishad* 3.14.1)

Advaita followers conventionally interpret these verses by equating the individual soul with the Supreme. They also equate the whole universe with Brahman (God), denying a Divine Personality distinct from it.

Ramanuja vehemently refuted this interpretation. He argued that these verses meant the individual soul is born from Brahman (God), resides in Brahman, and will merge back into Brahman, Who is all-pervading.

He illustrated using the analogy of a fish. Just like a fish is born from the ocean, lives in the ocean, and merges into the ocean, it does not mean that fish is the ocean. Similarly, the soul, a tiny fragment of God, cannot be the same as its Divine Creator.

Ramanuja also contended that the universe is not God per se but a manifestation of Him. He likened it to the many beads tied in one thread of a rosary. Similarly, the entire creation is bound together in a common thread of divinity, reflecting the presence of the Creator in every atom.

Debates turned into heated arguments between Ramanuja and

Yadav Prakash. Finally, the guru ordered his disciple to leave the gurukul. Ramanuja was now free to pursue his heart's calling of devotion to the Supreme Divine Personality.

Taking Refuge at the Feet of a Low Caste

Recognizing her son's devoutness, Ramanuja's mother suggested he make Kanchipurna his Guru. Though from a low caste, Kanchipurna was renowned amongst Yamunacharya's disciples for his fervent devotion.

For most spiritual teachers, having Ramanuja as a disciple would have been an honour. But, when Ramanuja sought refuge at Kanchipurna's feet, he initially refused, considering himself lowly and insignificant. Later, Kanchipurna had a divine inspiration after which he accepted Ramanuja as his disciple.

Both Kanchipurna and Ramanuja were householders. Ramanuja's wife was Rakshakambal. In those times, societal fanaticism was widespread and more prevalent in South India. Rakshakambal was an orthodox lady, proud of her status as a Brahmin. She, therefore, could not accept her husband's decision of accepting a low-caste person as his Guru.

Ramanuja thought that if he could somehow get the remnants of food eaten by Kanchipurna, he could rapidly progress on the spiritual path. He invited Kanchipurna over for a meal, intending to serve him personally and partake of his leftovers. The prescient Kanchipurna understood Ramanuja's intentions. In all his modesty, he could not think of giving away his leftovers. He tricked Ramanuja by arriving early at his house. Using the excuse of pending temple duties, he requested Ramanuja's wife for a quick meal.

The wife, though unhappy to receive a low-caste person at home, was bound by her husband's servitude to his Guru. So, she served the food but as soon as Kanchipurna left, she disdainfully picked up his plate with bamboo sticks and threw it in the dustbin. She then washed the entire room with water and also applied cow dung to disinfect it.

Mindless rituals get created by the ignorant in the name of spirituality. They forget that Shree Ram had lovingly accepted the half-eaten berries of a tribal lady, Shabari. Shree Krishna ate the banana peels lovingly offered by Vidurani. Even an iota of selfless devotion is immensely endearing to the Lord.

When Ramanuja returned home, he inquired about his Gurudev. His wife mentioned he had left after having his meal. Perplexed by Kanchipurna's swift arrival and departure, Ramanuja asked for his remnants as prasad. On learning how she had disgracefully discarded them, Ramanuja was furious. He chastised her for committing a grave sin against a noble soul and for being an encumbrance to his spiritual salvation. This incident deepened Ramanuja's detachment from his worldly relations.

The Divine Call and Initiation into Sanyas

When Ramanuja quit Yadav Prakash's gurukul, the news spread quickly and even reached Yamunacharya. He sent one of his senior disciples, Mahapurna, to bring Ramanuja to Srirangam.

When Ramanuja heard from Mahapurna about the order of the great Vaishnav Acharya, he got ready to proceed for Srirangam immediately. He did not even inform his wife, as he believed the Guru's position was above all else. However, little did he know of the huge disappointment that awaited him. When they reached Srirangam, it was too late—Yamunacharya had already taken mahasamadhi. He saw a group of disciples carrying the Acharya's body to the Kaveri River.

Ramanuja was overtaken by grief for not having met his Param-Guru. He looked at the lifeless body of Yamunacharya and sadly pondered over the missed opportunity. Just then, he noticed the Acharya's three fingers were closed. This was strange since a deceased person's fingers are always open, unlike a newborn whose fingers are tightly closed in a fist. Other disciples revealed that this was not Yamunacharya's normal hand posture.

Ramanuja comprehended that the closed fingers symbolized his Guru's three unfulfilled wishes. With divine guidance, he unflinchingly vowed to fulfil these:

1) To widely propagate Shri Vaishnav school of thought.
2) To write a commentary on the *Brahma Sutras*, establishing the supremacy of pure devotion and eternal service to the Lord.
3) To write a commentary on Nammalvar's most famous composition, *Tiruvaymoli*.

As Ramanuja loudly announced each resolve, one by one, Yamunacharya's closed fingers straightened out. The disciples understood that Ramanuja was blessed by their Guru. He then returned from Srirangam to Kanchipuram and absorbed himself even more in devotion. Consequently, tension with his wife, Rakshakambal, escalated at home, as Ramanuja had very little time for her.

Meanwhile, Yamunacharya's other disciples wondered why Ramanuja left Srirangam. They longed to associate with their new leader, who would carry forward the legacy of the departed Acharya. So, Mahapurna was sent again to bring Ramanuja back to Srirangam.

Mahapurna, along with his wife, arrived at Kanchipuram. Ramanuja was thrilled to receive them as he regarded Mahapurna as a fatherly figure. He invited the elderly couple to reside with him, giving them one-half of his house. Ramanuja lived in the other half with Rakshakambal, who loathed her husband's hospitality to his new guests.

For Ramanuja, the presence of Mahapurna was a blessing—a golden opportunity to deepen his learning of Shri Vaishnav philosophy. However, Ramanuja's devotion and gentle ways were increasingly in conflict with his wife's staunch orthodox practices.

One day, Rakshakambal and Mahapurna's wife were drawing water from the same well. Accidentally, some water from the latter's bucket spilled over into Rakshakambal's bucket. This served as a trigger for her pent-up emotions and unleashed her fury. Forgetting about etiquette towards her resident guest, Rakshakambal scolded Mahapurana's wife for 'polluting' the water meant for a Brahmin's household. The unassuming Mahapurna and his wife took this incident as a sign of Lord Ranganathaswamy calling them back to Srirangam.

On returning home that day, Ramanuja discovered what had transpired. Anguished beyond measure, he reprimanded

Rakshakambal for her narrow-mindedness and sent her to her parents' home. Subsequently, he adorned saffron robes, visited the temple of Lord Varadaraja Swamy and took sanyas, with the resolve to dedicate his life to the service of the Divine. Thenceforth, his name became *Yatiraj*, meaning 'chief among ascetics'.

This act caused a stir in the town of Kanchipuram. Many criticized Ramanuja for forsaking his householder life. However, his decision was not to escape from marital strife, rather a commitment to expand his family to include the whole world. He intended to address the welfare of all people—present and future—not just his bodily relatives.

As a renunciate, Ramanuja built his own ashram in Kanchipuram, which became a centre of spiritual and philosophical excellence. He now became famous as the great Ramanujacharya, whose reputation attracted many to seek his guidance.

The Move to Srirangam

In Srirangam, Yamunacharya's disciples were still awaiting Ramanujacharya's arrival to fill the void left by their great Guru. After much deliberation, they now orchestrated another plan to bring him back. They sent Yamunacharya's son to perform pooja at the temple of Lord Varadaraja Swamy at Kanchipuram during a festival. This son was exceptionally talented in presenting the Alvars' devotional poetry in dance form. The temple was packed with an eager audience to watch his performance. True to his reputation, he performed spectacularly, bringing joy to all present, including Ramanujacharya. Lord Varadaraja Swamy was so pleased that He ordained, through the chief priest, a boon of the artist's choice.

Yamunacharya's son expressed his desire to have Ramanujacharya in Srirangam permanently. Everyone present was dumbfounded. After a brief pause, Ramanujacharya bowed to Lord Varadaraja Swamy, seeking His permission to move to Srirangam to fulfil his life's purpose.

In Srirangam, Ramanujacharya was delighted to reunite with Mahapurna. He further studied the scriptures under Mahapurna and rendered great service to him. Following the prevalent tradition, Mahapurna encouraged Ramanuja to receive mantra diksha from Goshtipurna, a renowned disciple of Yamunacharya, who lived more than a hundred kilometres from Srirangam.

Ramanuja approached Goshtipurna 18 times, seeking wisdom and mantra diksha. Each time Goshtipurna refused to grace him. Despite this, Ramanuja remained determined, walking the hundred-mile journey back and forth on every trip. Finally, Goshtipurna agreed and initiated Ramanuja with the mantra *Om Namo Narayanaya*, with the condition that it would be kept secret, or else he would go to hell.

However, the magnanimous Ramanuja did not heed the consequences. He stood at the crossroads in the marketplace, announcing the secret mantra loudly to all. In his boundless compassion, he desired every soul to take Narayan's name and relish divine bliss.

When this news reached Goshtipurna, he reprimanded Ramanuja for such a blatant violation of his order. However, Ramanuja politely replied that if the mantra had the potency to bestow welfare, why should everyone not benefit from it? And he was ready to accept any punishment, including going to hell, for the greater good of humankind.

Moved by Ramanuja's noble intentions, Goshtipurna joyfully embraced him and declared him as a true preacher of God. Ramanuja now came to be called Lakshman. Goshtipurna also blessed Ramanuja with widespread fame and bestowed him the name *Emperumanar*, meaning 'more compassionate than God'.

Back in Srirangam, Ramanujacharya reformed the operations of the Ranganathaswamy Temple—the largest and most important Vishnu temple in South India. The holy shrine had fallen into the hands of a malicious priest, who was merely garnering power and wealth, in the name of temple duties. Ramanujacharya tactfully resolved all administrative issues. He also enforced ritualistic procedures as prescribed in the Agam shastras.

These reformatory steps incensed priests who had been fudging rituals and malingering duties. Resentfully, they plotted to kill Ramanujacharya. On one occasion, he was given poisoned *charanamrit* (sacred water after washing the Lord's feet). However, it had no effect on him. This bewildered the priests. Instead of realizing Ramanujacharya's divinity, they tried harder to get rid of him.

The pujaris got a lady to offer him poisoned *bhiksha* (food offering given to a sanyasi). The Acharya carried the *bhiksha* to a river and placed it on the bank while he did his midday ablutions. As luck would have it, a bird and a dog consumed it and died.

Ramanujacharya realized the priests' intention to eliminate him as a response to his temple reforms. Undisturbed, he simply ceased accepting *bhiksha* and retreated to Thiruvellarai, a nearby *Divya Desam*, for a few days.

The Divine Sibling Bond

Ramanujacharya used to worship Andal—the great woman saint in the Alvar tradition. He used to recite Andal's hymns, particularly her verses from the *Nachiyar Thirumozhi*. On one such occasion, Ramanujacharya was fervently singing a *pasuram* (verse) *Naaru Narum Polil*.

The *pasuram* expresses Andal's desire to offer 108 vessels of rice payasam (a sweet dish made with rice, milk, ghee, jaggery, and spices) to Lord Sundararaja of Thirumalirumcholai. Andal had desired to please Lord Sundararaja and obtain His blessing to get married to Lord Ranganathaswamy.

While singing the *pasuram*, Ramanujacharya contemplated deeply on Andal's heartfelt sentiment and wondered if she was able to fulfil her desire. Subsequently, he took it upon himself to act on it. On Andal's behalf, he offered the prasad of butter and rice payasam in 108 vessels in the Sundararaja Perumal Temple. Thereafter, Ramanujacharya journeyed to Srivilliputhur, Andal's birthplace, where She is enshrined with Lord Ranganathaswamy.

As he entered Andal's temple, he was surprised to find that Andal's deity had stepped forward as if awaiting his arrival. She greeted him as *Anna* (elder brother), acknowledging the loving act he had performed on her behalf at Thirumalirumcholai.

To this day, in the Srivilliputhur temple, the Goda Devi (Andal) deity is seen positioned two steps forward, commemorating this divine encounter of the two Saintly personalities. Since then, Ramanujacharya was conferred the title *Godagraja*, meaning 'Godai's elder brother'. Andal came to be known as *Yathiraja Sahodari*, meaning 'sister of Ramanujacharya'.

During his recitation of Andal's other famed composition, *Thiruppavai*, Ramanujacharya used to deliver enthralling sermons expounding on the profound depths of its verses. Consequently, he was honoured with the title of *Thiruppavai Jeeyar*. From then on, devotees chant *Om Goda Agrajaya Namaha* while praying to Ramanujacharya and *Om Yathiraja Sahodaryai Nama* while praying to Goda Devi, emphasizing their eternal brother-sister bond.

Fulfilling His Vows

Ramanujacharya authored nine books, known as the *Navratna*, among which three are particularly renowned. One is *Vedartha Sangraha*, which gives insights into the Upanishads. The second is *Gita Bhashya*, an extensive illustration of Yamunacharya's *Geethartha Sangraha*.

The third is the magnum opus of Shri Vaishnavite literature—*Shree Bhashya*. This is a commentary on the *Brahma Sutras* written to fulfil the solemn promise he had made to Yamunacharya. Having completed it, to gather support for his commentary, Ramanujacharya travelled to Kashmir. It was an important seat of learning in that era. The scholars of Kashmir admired his masterful explanations. They honoured Ramanujacharya with a symbol of *Hayagriva* (horse-headed avatar of Vishnu). This symbol is visible even today in Ramanujacharya's birthplace, Sriperumbudur.

Ramanujacharya also wrote *Vedanta Dipa* for novice spiritual aspirants. Additionally, he expressed the key principles of his compositions in *Sharanagati Gadya*. Further, he dedicated a devotional work, *Sriranga Gadya*, to Lord Ranganathaswamy, in which he seeks eternal servitude.

Ramanujacharya widely disseminated Shri Vaishnav principles. One of his exceptionally capable disciples wrote a commentary on *Nachiyar Tiruvaymozhi*. Through these endeavours, Ramanujacharya fulfilled all three vows he had made to his ultimate Guru, Yamunacharya.

Living His Teachings of Bhakti, Service, and Equality

Ramanuja's heart was deeply drawn to Lord Varadaraja Swamy in Kanchipuram, experiencing profound and unconditional love for Him. He encouraged people to actively participate in temple services, such as cleaning, gathering flowers, singing bhajans, reading scriptures, and so on.

Ramanujacharya became the proponent of the *Vishishta Advaita* philosophy. He believed that the Almighty has numerous divine Attributes and Forms. Bhagavan Narayan is the supreme amongst these Forms. He resides eternally in Vaikuntha, His divine Abode.

The soul, although a distinct conscious entity, is inseparable from God. It is eternally subservient to the Supreme Almighty. Communion with the Divine is achieved only through exclusive self-surrender and undivided devotion.

This philosophy sharply differed from the popular understanding of Shankaracharya's *Advaita* philosophy, which did not distinguish between God and His tiny fragment—the materially bound souls.

Ramanujacharya established that jiva (soul), *jagat* (world), and God are three fundamental truths. While Shankaracharya termed *jagat* as *mithya* (false), Ramanujacharya stated that since God created the world, it cannot be false. He likened the relationship between the universe and God to that between the Sun and its rays. Accordingly, jiva and *jagat* are also integral parts of God, not illusions.

Ramanujacharya advised people to have faith in the teachings of the Vedas and the great Saints, and to always remain in the company of those devoted to God. He warned against becoming a slave of one's senses. The primary enemies on the path to God-realization, he stressed, were desire, anger, and greed.

Challenging events are often woven into the lives of Saints, which naturally reflect the strength and purity of their devotion. Ramanujacharya's life was threatened by many, including priestly authorities and his own first teacher, Yadav Prakash. Despite realizing their ill intentions, Ramanuja never became distressed. Rather, he was so large-hearted that he continued in their association with the hope of transforming them onto the right path. No wonder Ramanujacharya took sanyas for the greater good of society, including the people who hated him. The Ramayan states:

> sant hṛiday navanīt samānā,
>   kahā kabinh pari kahai na jānā   (Uttar Kand 7.124.4)

The heart of saintly people is so soft that they become sad on seeing others suffer, while they are happy on seeing others rejoice. Hence, even at the cost of personal loss, they help others.

Human relationships are complex matters requiring sacrifice, adjustment, and understanding for their sustenance. Ramanujacharya's only intention was to serve, which is why he was never heartbroken on seeing others' weaknesses. Instead, he saw it as his duty to help them overcome their frailties. Is there a way we can also nurture such an attitude to serve? Yes! If we can perfect our service attitude towards God, we will then look to serve in everything we do. We will view others as God's children and act accordingly to please our Beloved Lord. Then, with detachment and compassion, we will be able to harmoniously navigate relationships.

Ramanujacharya's universal teachings on devotion and equality of all living beings transformed even his detractors. The growing list of followers of Ramanujacharya included Yadav Prakash, who took the order of sanyas from his own former disciple.

Like Shankaracharya, Ramanujacharya also undertook a *digvijayi yatra* (victory march), travelling extensively across Bharat to spread bhakti yog. He visited almost all sacred places, including Kashi, Kashmir, and Badrinath. During his travels, he organized a network of temples dedicated to the worship of Lakshmi Narayan, with standardized rituals. He also established *mathas* (centres) for *Vishishta Advaita* studies.

After extensively travelling through the length and breadth of the land, Ramanujacharya returned to Srirangam, where he settled permanently to continue his prachar and write books.

Thousands would come to hear his lectures. He instilled the seva bhav in all working in the temples, established standard practices for all rituals, and corrected many social evils that had pervaded society.

In those days, temples were the hubs of knowledge, employment, and culture. However, these important nerve centres of society were controlled by a particular social group. Hence, not everyone who desired to serve the Lord in the temple was allowed to do so. The downtrodden were even banned from entering the temple, accused of polluting the sacred premises. But Ramanujacharya did not subscribe to discrimination based on caste. Due to his magnanimity and compassion, the temple doors were opened for people from all sections of society. According to him, the only qualification for entry into the temple was love and devotion for the Lord in the heart. He encouraged inclusiveness by allotting 50 per cent of services in the temple to the non-brahmin castes. Further, though some Alvars were from lower castes, their devotional songs were made mandatory in the temples.

With all such reforms, Ramanujacharya conveyed a clear message that everyone belongs to the Lord, irrespective of caste and profession. He believed that being a brahmin is not determined by birth but by one's actions. In his ashram too, he accepted disciples from all castes and made no distinctions in imparting knowledge. In an era where women did not have access to education, he created learning centres for them. Ramanujacharya was thus a great social reformer. His advocacy for inclusivity and upliftment of marginalized communities endeared him to the masses.

With his inspiration, countless people turned to the path of true bhakti. He had a congregation of 700 sanyasis and nominated 74 acharyas to hold special responsibilities in the *mathas* to succeed him. In recognition of his scholasticism and devotion, through which he steered a spiritual revolution, he was honoured with the title of *Jagadguru*. The title reflected his status as a teacher whose wisdom transcended regional boundaries and applied to the entire world.

Samadhi

It is believed that Ramanujacharya lived for 120 years. One version states that his body is still preserved inside the Shri Ranganathaswamy Temple in Srirangam. His devotees see him as the descension of *Anant Shesh*, the divine serpent upon whom Lord Vishnu rests.

9

Purandara Dasa

Purandara Dasa was a highly gifted and talented devotee of Shree Krishna in the sixteenth century. Though born into riches, he underwent a deep transformation, renouncing all his wealth to embrace a life of devotion and piety. He was a prominent proponent of the Haridasa tradition espousing the sentiment of 'servant of the Lord' and dedicated his life to preaching love for God and righteous living.

Sant Purandara Dasa is revered as the *Pitamaha* (grandfather) of Carnatic music, having composed an astounding 475,000 bhajans. His mastery of poetry and music was so profound that his words would spontaneously emanate as devotional songs. As a result, he is often called the *Uttampadkarta*, or 'superlative composer'.

His devotional music and wisdom have touched the lives of countless devotees. His compositions, known as *padas* and *devarunamas*, are primarily in simple Kannada and sometimes in Sanskrit. These songs encapsulate themes of devotion, morality, good conduct, and empathy. Through simple hymns, Purandara taught abstract Vedic principles to the masses. This is why his devotees also refer to his works as *Purandara Upanishad*.

Birth and Early Life

Sant Purandara Dasa was born in AD 1484 in Araga, a town under the Vijayanagar empire. It corresponds to Thirthalli in modern-day Karnataka. He was born to an affluent jeweller merchant couple, Varadappa Nayak and Lakshmibai (Rukmini). Believing he came to them as a blessing of Lord Venkateshwar, his parents named him Srinivasa.

Srinivasa Nayak was a bright student and quickly mastered many scriptures, Sanskrit, Kannada, and music. Though scholarly, he was uninterested in spirituality, being fascinated by material wealth and possessions. At 16, his parents got him married to a pious lady, Saraswati Bai.

When Srinivasa was only 20, his father passed away. Now, the responsibility of the jewellery business fell on Srinavasa's shoulders. With a lustful zeal for prosperity, he dedicated his time to expanding the business. As a result, he accumulated wealth beyond imagination. In fact, biographers estimate he amassed riches that would even surpass the fortunes of the billionaire tycoons of today. This earned him the title of *Navakoti Narayan*, meaning 'lord of unsurpassed wealth'.

Years went by earning money, yet Srinivasa's obsession with material opulence did not subside. Though incredibly wealthy, he was an extreme miser and had no interest in charitable work. Saraswati Bai, as a dutiful wife, tried to grapple with her husband's stinginess. However, God had a different plan. He knew of Srinivasa's inherent virtues and divine mission, so He orchestrated a leela (pastime) to bring forth Srinivasa's transformation.

Shree Krishna Revives Srinivasa Nayak's Devotional Sanskars

A popular legend states that God took the form of a poor brahmin and came to Srinivasa Nayak's shop. He requested Srinivasa for money for his son's *Upanayana* (sacred thread ceremony). The stingy and parsimonious Srinivasa would repeatedly turn the brahmin away.

This continued for six months, after which the Lord approached Saraswati Bai. He knew of her generous heart and explained Srinivasa's unwillingness to help. Saraswati Bai was deeply embarrassed at her husband's behaviour but had no access to her husband's wealth. She said to the Lord in the guise of the brahmin, 'Swamy, I have nothing to give you.'

The brahmin responded, 'Your nose ring was a gift from your mother. Can you offer it for my son's *Upanayana*?' Saraswati Bai did not think twice and promptly placed the precious nose ring in His hands.

The brahmin took the nose ring to Srinivasa's shop. Nayak was annoyed to see the brahmin return and chided him saying, 'Why do you keep pestering me? I have told you I cannot give you any charity.'

The brahmin remarked, 'I am not here to beg for alms. Kindly give me a loan, and keep this nose ring as collateral.'

Srinivasa inspected the nose ring carefully and immediately recognized it as his wife's. Alarmed, he asked, 'Where did you get this?'

'A generous soul gave it to me,' the brahmin responded.

Srinivasa said, 'I need time to evaluate the ring, so please come back tomorrow.'

Nayak hurried home and questioned his wife regarding the whereabouts of her nose ring. He demanded to see it. However, Saraswati Bai had already given it away; there was no way she could produce it. And if Srinivasa were to find out the truth that she had donated the nose ring, he would surely punish her. She felt petrified, thinking of the punishment that awaited her.

Fearing her husband's wrath, Saraswati Bai decided to end her life. Entering her room, she poured poison into a cup. As she was about to drink, she heard a metallic sound. To her astonishment, her nose ring lay at the bottom of the cup. She threw away the poison and ran to give the ring to her husband.

Now, it was Srinivasa's turn to be shocked. He had placed this ornament in his shop vault, so how could it be in two places? The next morning, the very first thing he did on entering the shop was to check the vault. To his utmost amazement, the nose ring was missing. The mystery was thickening!

As requested, the brahmin came back and asked Srinivasa to disburse the loan. Srinivasa quietly gave the money. He then instructed his assistant to follow the brahmin to learn of his whereabouts. The assistant came back to report that the brahmin had entered the temple and disappeared.

Srinivasa understood that the brahmin was none other than Vitthal Bhagavan Shree Krishna, the presiding deity of the famous Pandharpur temple. He was Srinivasa Nayak's *Iṣhṭa Dev*. The same Merciful One, Who gives freely to all, had come to him for alms, and Srinivasa had denied Him.

Srinivasa repented his harsh miserliness. Despite possessing knowledge of the Vedas, he had not put it to practice. His wife, though uneducated, was clearly more spiritual, as she had behaved with immaculate generosity and kindness. Srinivasa felt guilty about his unbecoming behaviour to Vitthal Bhagavan and was steeped in shame.

The divine encounter with Shree Krishna led to a complete transformation in Srinivasa's life. The pendulum of his inner consciousness swung from gross materialism to intense spirituality. He declared to his family that they would now live as *Haridasas*—dedicating their life to singing bhajans and serving God.

He donated all his wealth to the needy, keeping not a broken nickel for himself. Shree Krishna had touched Srinivasa Nayak's heart and changed him forever. The former miserly merchant now began his journey towards becoming the magnanimous Purandara Dasa.

Turning Point—Srinivasa's Inner Awakening

Srinivasa had begun a new chapter in his life. He became a follower of the Haridasa Sampradaya, a sect from Madhvacharya's lineage that propagates love for God through singing bhajans. Haridasas are mendicant devotees who travel from city to city while chanting on the streets.

Srinivasa took a tanpura in his hand and began singing kirtans on the roads. The neck that once adorned resplendent gold necklaces was now decorated with a tulsi mala. And the man who was once the richest in the land was now subsisting on alms for a living. He had left everything and placed all his faith in the shelter of his Beloved Lord.

What an amazing inner awakening of Srinivasa's *jnana chakshu* (eyes of knowledge). Where he once differentiated based on lucre and designations, he now saw all as the children of God. No longer in his eyes was anyone big or small; they were all one with Shree Krishna. This equanimity of vision is the sign of a true pandit:

> mātṛivatparadāreṣhu paradravyeṣhu loṣhṭravat
> ātmavatsarvabhūteṣhu yaḥ paśhyati sa paṇḍitaḥ
> (Chanakya Neeti 12.14)

'One who views another's wife as his mother and sees others' wealth as mud. One who considers all living beings as his own; such a person perceives the world rightly and is a true pandit.'

How can we all learn to look at the world with such equanimity? To uplift our perspective, we must grow in knowledge. At present, faulty knowledge distorts our perception of things. Selfishness predominates our thoughts, and we believe that the world must fulfil all our desires. When things do not go as we wish, we become upset. We miss the reality that we exist for the sake of the Universe and not the other way around.

The Vedic scriptures are called *Darshan Shastras*, 'books that enable one to see'. They equip us with divine wisdom to see the world as it is. Our values, beliefs, and priorities get transformed by the inner awakening. Then, through the *jnana chakṣhu*, or eyes of knowledge, we perceive things as they truly are. As the Hindi saying goes:

> dṛiṣhṭi badalne se sṛishti badaltī hai

'If you change the way you look at the world, the world changes for you.' Srinivasa now saw the entire world as belonging to Vitthal and himself as a servant of Vitthal.

Detachment—Developing Dispassion Is Vital in Spirituality

Srinivasa was now living an enlightened life. As a Haridasa, he displayed extreme detachment from material possessions and pursuits. He decided to visit Hampi, the capital of Vijayanagar, to meet the great saint, Vyas Teerth, who resided there. The entire family decided to undertake this journey to pay their respects to the great sage.

On the way was a dense forest fraught with danger from bandits. As they got closer, Saraswati Bai grew anxious. Srinivasa questioned why she was worried when they had no material possessions with them. Saraswati Bai confessed she still had a small golden vessel. Without hesitation, Srinivasa took the vessel and tossed it into the foliage. Saraswati Bai was instantly relieved, and they continued their journey to Hampi with a free mind.

In tossing away the last of his gold belongings, Srinivasa had expressed his complete indifference to material wealth. He had discovered the profound truth about worldly riches. No matter how much one possesses, there is never any fulfilment, for one always continues to strive for more.

This is the destination disease—one believes a destination ahead will give happiness while the journey passes without happiness, in anticipation of future bliss. When the goal is attained, there is momentary joy, but then again discontentment sets in and the cycle repeats itself. It is like chasing a mirage in the desert, which always promises contentment, yet never delivers it. The *Garuḍ Puran* states:

> *chakradharo 'pi suratvam*
>   *suratvalābhe sakalasurapatitvam*
> *bhavtium surapatirūrdhvagatitvam*
>   *tathāpi nanivartate tṛiṣhṇā*   (2.12.14)

'A king wishes to be emperor of the world; the emperor aspires to be a celestial being. The celestial being seeks to be Indra, the king of heaven; and Indra desires to be Brahma, the creator. Yet the thirst for material enjoyment does not get satiated.'

Detachment is fundamental to progress on the spiritual path, for it turns the mind away from material allurements. Then, one comes in touch with the inner bliss of the soul and becomes transcendentally situated.

So, how does one become detached? We must begin by cultivating knowledge about our 'real self', which is the soul, a tiny fragment of the Supreme Soul. Presently, we consider ourselves to be the body. Thus, we seek to relish bliss from the world—people, places, and things. These material pleasures are fleeting and leave our soul unsatisfied. This implies our happiness lies beyond the mundane.

The holy scriptures point us in the direction of lasting happiness. They elucidate that we are the soul, which is not material but divine. Hence, the happiness we seek is also divine. The source of this divine joy is God. He is the Ocean of Infinite Bliss. As His fragments, we experience true happiness by getting closer to Him.

Inculcating this belief changes our perspective on life. Instead of material allurements, spiritual treasures become our goal. We realize all the things we previously thought important—professional success, financial gains, and social prestige—will be left behind one day. But spiritual assets are permanent and continue with us after death. With this clarity, we begin to turn towards God. Then, we grow in devotion, spiritual wisdom, and selfless love. Srinivasa Nayak was a blazing example of such a transformation.

Srinivasa Meets His Guru and Is Ordained as Saint Purandara Dasa

Srinivasa soon arrived in Hampi. Vyas Teerth, a renowned guru of the Madhvacharya Sampradaya resided there. He was a great scholar and devotee of Shree Krishna. Guruji welcomed Srinivasa wholeheartedly, saying, 'Come. I have been expecting you. Now, you are my disciple. From today, you will be called Purandara Dasa.'

He now had a spiritual name received from his Gurudev. *Purandara Dasa* literally means 'servant of Shree Krishna'. However, his Guru added another epithet to it: 'You are the servant of the servants, *dāson ke dāsa*, Purandara Dasa.'

Vyas Teerth first taught Purandara the codes of conduct to be followed by laypersons and householders. Next, he taught Haridasa philosophy and devotion to God. After this, he ordained Purandara to integrate this knowledge into his bhajans, through which he could propagate the path of bhakti. Purandara also went on to sign his compositions as *Purandara Vittala*.

Sant Purandara Dasa is considered the foremost amongst the Harisdasas, so much so that his Guru praised him, saying, 'If one is a dasa, he should be like Purandara Dasa.' There are very few disciples who are praised by their own teacher. Such is the legacy and stature of Purandara Dasa.

Purandara Begins Composing Bhajans and Disseminating Knowledge

Purandara began composing and singing poetry in simple Kannada that would be easy for the masses to understand. His spontaneous utterances would take the form of beautiful songs. He profusely glorified the Supreme in many forms, such as Shree Krishna, Ram, Vitthal, Venkateshwar, and Vishnu. In the history of humankind, no other composer has been more prolific. The total number of his bhajans reached an unimaginable 475,000!

Through his compositions, Purandara delved into many themes. Naturally, as a Saint, his favourite topic was devotion and the Leelas of God. However, he also urged people to cultivate the virtues of kindness, generosity, forgiveness, and discipline. Let us savour one such bhajan.

> *rāgi tandīryā bhikṣhake, rāgi tandīryā,*
> *yogyarāgi, bhogyarāgi,*
>   *bhāgyavantarāgi nīvu*
>
> *annadānava māḍuvarāgi*
>   *anna chatra vaniṭṭavarāgi,*
>   *anya vārteyagala biṭṭavarāgi,*
>   *anudina bhajaneya māḍuvarāgi*

mātā pitarannu sevipaāgi,
　pāpa kāryava biṭṭavarāgi,
rīthiya bālanu bāluvarāgi,
　nīti mārgadali khyātarāgi

guru kāruṇyava paḍedavarāgi
　guru vākhyavannu pāliparāgi,
guruvina pādava smarisuvarāgi,
　parama puṇyava māḍuvarāgi

kāma krodhava aḷidavarāgi,
　nema nishtegala māḍuvarāgi,
rama nāmava japisuvarāgi,
　premadi kuṇikuṇidāḍuvarāgi

siri ramaṇa sadā smarisuvarāgi,
　guruvige bāgovanthavarāgi,
kare kare bhavavanu nīguvararāgi,
　purandara viṭṭalana seviparāgi

'Have you brought *rāgi* (millet) to give alms? May you be an upright person. May you feed others, establish inns, and give free food. May you not bother with other matters. But may you only sing the Name of God daily. May you serve your father and mother.

May you forsake sinful actions. May you lead a disciplined life and be famous for just actions. May you be one who gets your Guru's grace and obeys the words of the Guru. May you contemplate on the feet of the Guru, and may you be the one doing blessed deeds.

May you forsake passion and anger, perform rituals according to rules, and keep on chanting the name of Ram. And may you dance out of pure love. May you always think of Lakshmi, bow before the Guru, and forsake sinful deeds. May you be one who serves Purandara Vittala.'

To fulfil his Guru's wish, Purandara began travelling from place to place. He did this for 15 years, singing the glories of Bhagavan and spreading divine wisdom. Later, he returned to Hampi and settled down—again taking to the streets with nupur on his feet and tanpura in his hands, chanting for the pleasure of his Lord.

Purandara Dasa Teaches Meaning of True Wealth

As a true Haridasa, Purandara lived by the principle of minimalism. His complete detachment from material wealth is illustrated in the following two incidents from his life.

Once Saraswati Bai's relatives visited their home. To make arrangements, she borrowed a golden utensil from the neighbours, which she sold to fund the gathering. Purandara returned home, and seeing the feast, wondered where the money had come from. Saraswati explained her actions and the loan they would have to repay.

Purandara was very displeased. He argued she should have been honest about their circumstances instead of creating an unnecessary façade. Hearing his words, the guests felt humiliated and left. The neighbours, too, were annoyed that their golden vessel had been sold.

To resolve the issue, Purandara instructed his son to take a dip in the pond. The lad then emerged from the pond with four golden utensils. One was duly returned to the neighbour, and the matter was resolved. This miraculous event left everyone in awe.

Krishnadevaraya, ruler of the Vijaynagar empire, was a renowned king in Indian history. He was impressed by Purandara Dasa's devotion and simplicity and supported him in various ways. The king gave wealth to Purandara Dasa. However, the Saint gave it all in charity by distributing it to the needy and did not keep anything for his family or himself.

The king was surprised and questioned Purandara about it, especially because he was living in abject poverty. Purandara Dasa recapitulated his history, 'Earlier, I had far more wealth than you. People called me *Navakoti Narayan*. Today, I possess assets which cannot be seen with the eyes. The treasure I have cannot be stolen by thieves, nor will it rust with moisture. My wealth is divine love. What can you give me that is more valuable than it?'

Saints worldwide emphasize love for God as true wealth. Saint Kabir states:

> *kabīrā sab jag nirdhanā dhanvantā nahiṅ koy*
> *dhanvantā soi jāniye jāhi prem dhan hoy*

'Everyone is poor in this world; no one is rich. Know that person alone to be wealthy who possesses the treasure of love for God.' Purandara may have been poor in the eyes of the king, but he was rich in the eyes of God.

Meeting of Two Esteemed Saints

One of the sweetest occurrences in bhakti is the meeting of two saints. We can learn so much from the manner in which they venerate and shower affection on each other. Imagine, then, the interaction between two epoch-making saints of the bhakti era!

Purandara Dasa was a fervent devotee of the deity Vitthal Shree Krishna. One of his contemporaries was Annamacharya, a great Telugu poet-saint and devotee of Lord Venkateshwar. Annamacharya was older than Purandara Dasa, but they shared many commonalities in their work and impact—both were famous saints, prolific bhajan writers, and stalwarts of devotional bhakti music.

The saints once met and expressed deep reverence for each other. They profusely praised each other's spiritual eminence. Purandara Dasa eulogized Annamacharya by saying he was the personification of Lord Venkateshwar Himself. Likewise, Annamacharya revered Purandara Dasa as the embodiment of Lord Vitthal. In this way, there was a loving and heartfelt exchange between the two great devotees.

God Graces Purandara in Numerous Ways and Brightens His Love

Purandara Dasa was blessed with multiple divine encounters and graces. One astonishing incident occurred when he accompanied Guru Vyasa Teerth and King Krishnadevaraya to Tirupati for the darshan of Lord Venkateshwar. Some devotees joined them, and Purandara Dasa was responsible for arranging their meals and ensuring everyone was fed.

Purandara instructed his disciple, Appanna, to purchase ghee, but the latter forgot. In a wondrous turn of events, God Himself manifested as Appanna and brought the ghee. The disciple later returned and apologized for his mistake. Purandara realized the divine intervention—the Lord had come to help him serve the devotees. He was utterly humbled and grateful at the immense display of compassion of his Beloved Vitthal.

In a subsequent occurrence, Appanna forgot to bring some pooja materials. This infuriated Purandara, and he slapped his disciple. Later, at the Vitthal Mandir, he found that Bhagavan's cheek was swollen. The message was very clear. The Lord had admonished him, saying, 'You slapped My devotee. Look! I bore the consequence of that slap. Why did you slap him?'

Filled with remorse, Purandara Dasa deeply regretted his actions, and the swelling on Vitthal Bhagavan's cheek subsided. However, an unusual incident soon ensued.

Commotion took place in town as news spread that Lord Vitthal's precious bracelet was missing. It was later found with a dancer, who was accused of theft. The chief priest of the temple was furious. He questioned the dancer as to how the bracelet came to be in her possession. At first, she denied stealing the bracelet but later alleged, 'Purandara Dasa gave it to me.'

The priest was alarmed and exclaimed, 'Purandara Dasa gave it to you? We thought he was a noble saint!'

Now, Purandara was summoned and interrogated. He vehemently refuted the accusation. But no one believed him. The priests declared the punishment—both Purandara and the dancer should be tied to the temple pillar and whipped. As the lashes began to fall pitiably on the Saint, Purandara realized the play of God. This was Bhagavan Vitthal's retribution for the swollen cheek that Purandara had caused. As the Ramayan states:

> karam pradhān viśhv kari rākhā
> jo jas karai so tas phalu chākhā

'This world is regulated by the Law of Karma. Whatever you do, you will inevitably reap its consequences.' Purandara had caused pain to the Lord and was made to pay for it.

After a few lashes, a voice spoke from the temple altar. Vitthal Bhagavan declared, 'Purandara Dasa did not steal the bracelet; stop whipping him.'

The priest and other devotees felt deeply remorseful and begged Purandara's forgiveness. The great Saint compassionately forgave them, knowing that Lord Vitthal had orchestrated this ordeal for his purification.

These episodes from Purandara Dasa's life are a testament to his inextinguishable love for God. Every encounter reveals the Saint's rich sentiments of faith and surrender, serving as beautiful learnings for all.

Purandara Dasa Epitomized Kirtan as the Life and Soul of Devotion

Purandara used bhajan as a medium for preaching and *jiva kalyan* (welfare of the souls). He had set an extraordinary personal goal for his life—to compose 500,000 bhajans. By the age of 80, he had written an amazing 475,000 songs, yet fell short of his goal by 25,000.

Purandara Dasa lived till the age of 80. Legend states he left his body through *jal* samadhi by entering the Tungabhadra River behind the Vijay Vittal temple in Hampi. What happened to his resolve of writing 500,000 bhajans? Some say Purandara requested his son, Madhvapati, to complete the remaining compositions. Since he lacked his father's divine inspiration, Madhvapati felt unworthy and declined this monumental task. Instead, he urged Purandara to return in another life to complete the remaining bhajans. Some believe that Purandara Dasa reincarnated as Vijay Dasa and fulfilled his promise by composing the final 25,000 bhajans.

Today, most of his compositions are lost, leaving only a fraction for devotees to cherish. Regardless, the remaining bhajans are a blazing testament to his devotion. Additionally, Purandara greatly contributed to Indian classical music. He presented a systematic method of teaching Carnatic music with *swaravalis* and *alankars*, which is followed even today. He introduced the raga 'Maya Malava Gowla' as the fundamental scale for musical instruction. He composed numerous *geetams* (songs with simple melody), of which only a few are extant. The *Pillari Geeta* composed in raga Malahari is one such example. It is an invocatory composition in praise of Lord Ganesh, Shiv, and other deities, rendered when beginning anything auspicious. It is also considered a good starting point for novice learners of Carnatic music.

Purandara Dasa's innovative music style also profoundly influenced succeeding composers, including the legendary Tyagaraja. It is documented that Saint Tyagaraja, born centuries later, revered Purandara Dasa as his *manasic guru* (spiritual mentor in the mind), a sentiment instilled in him by his mother.

The Vedic scriptures particularly extol kirtan as a simple and profound way of deeply connecting with God in the age of Kali. The Shreemad Bhagavatam states:

> kṛite yad dhyāyato viṣhṇum tretāyām yajato makhaiḥ
> dwāpare paricharyāyām kalau tad dhari-kīrtanāt
>
> (12.3.52)

'The best process of devotion in the age of Satya was simple meditation upon God. In the age of *Tretā*, it was the performance of sacrifices for the pleasure of God. In the age of *Dwāpar*, worship of the deities was the recommended process. In the present age of Kali, it is kirtan alone.'

The *Bhakti Rasamrit Sindhu* defines kirtan as:

> nāma-līlā-guṇadīnām uchchair-bhāṣhā tu kīrtanam
>
> (1.2.145)

'Singing glories of the Abodes, Associates, Names, Forms, Pastimes, and Qualities of God is called kirtan.' It involves the three-fold processes of:

- shravan (hearing),
- kirtan (chanting), and
- smaran (remembering).

The goal is to fix the mind upon God. Hearing and chanting are highly effective when done together with remembering. They charm the senses and when the mind starts to wander, they gently guide it back. Besides, kirtans are replete with prayers, glories of God, and divine wisdom. Dwelling on their meaning becomes an aid for contemplation and meditation.

Another benefit of kirtan is that it helps block out distracting sounds, fostering increased concentration. And since kirtan involves loud chanting, the divine vibrations of the Names of God make the entire environment auspicious and holy.

For all these reasons, kirtan has been the most popular form of devotion among saints in Indian history. All the great poet-saints composed numerous devotional songs, and through them, they engaged in chanting, hearing, and remembering.

Today, we fondly acclaim Purandara Dasa as a legendary composer who enriched bhakti literature through the timeless beauty of devotional music. One can derive great spiritual benefits by cherishing the invaluable treasure chest of his compositions.

10

Vallabhacharya

Vallabhacharya was an exceptional philosopher in the annals of Indian history, a powerful preacher, and an exclusive devotee of Shree Krishna. His approach to spirituality was exceedingly sublime—he perceived Shree Krishna everywhere and guided his followers to do the same. Along with a heart full of devotion, he also possessed profound scholarly prowess. With every sermon and episode in his life, Vallabh won the hearts of countless devotees.

Vallabhacharya is revered as the founder of Pushti Marg (Path of Grace). It emphasizes cultivating bhakti through the grace of God. Its underlying philosophy is known as *Shuddha Advaita vada* (Pure Non-Dualism), which is one of the five major schools of Vedant in India.

Vallabhacharya undertook three long pilgrimages across India to spread his gospel of divine love. He preferred a simple life—travelling on foot, donning plain attire, and preparing his own meals. To avoid crowds, particularly those seeking material boons, he would reside on the outskirts of villages.

During his travels, Vallabhacharya propagated Shree Krishna bhakti by lecturing on sacred texts, such as the Bhagavad Gita and Shreemad Bhagavatam. The sites where he delivered discourses became known as *baithaks* (seats). Eighty-four of these exist and are scattered across India, with several in Gujarat and Rajasthan. The devotees of Pushti Marg revere these *baithaks* as sacred shrines of their founder.

Birth and Early Childhood

Vallabhacharya appeared in 1479 CE in the forest of Champaranya, currently in Chhattisgarh, India. His parents, Laxman Bhatt and Illammagaru Devi, lived in Kankarwad on the banks of the Krishna River in present-day Andhra Pradesh. When Illammagaru was pregnant, the couple desired to raise their future child in Kashi (Varanasi). With this intention, they undertook a pilgrimage to the holy city. However, the political situation in Kashi turned perilous due to the Mohammedan invasions. So, the couple fled the city.

While they were in the forest of Champaranya, Illammagaru, who was seven months pregnant, delivered her baby prematurely. The infant was minuscule and appeared lifeless. The parents assumed the child to be stillborn. Leaving the infant in the forest, they continued their journey.

As destiny would have it, they received news that the political situation in Kashi had stabilized. Returning to Kashi, they arrived at the same spot where they had left the baby three days earlier. To their amazement, they found the infant alive, surrounded by a protective ring of fire. Their joy knew no bounds. The mother picked up her child and held him tightly against her chest. They named the child *Vallabh*, meaning 'the beloved one', which he indeed was—not only to his parents but also to God.

Laxman Bhatt settled down in Kashi and began arranging the best of religious education for Vallabh. In the city of scholars, young Vallabh was exposed to the philosophies of great Acharyas and the teachings of all the scriptures. Consequently, at a young age itself, he became proficient in the Vedas, Puranas, and the Agam shastras.

Simultaneously, Vallabh was drawn to Krishna bhakti. The Krishna Leela paintings in his home captivated his imagination, especially the *Raas Leela*. He would spend hours gazing at the portrait, engrossed in deep contemplation.

Vallabh's Philosophy: *Shuddha Advaita Vada* (Pure Non-Dualism)

While still young, Vallabh's philosophic concepts began crystallizing into a profound doctrine. Though Kashi was dominated by *Advaita* ideology, Vallabh felt it was too dry and intellectual for commoners. Furthermore, it sidelined love for God. Vallabh sought to revive devotion and bring it to the forefront of all spiritual practices. Declaring himself as a *Krishna Das*, he advocated bhakti as a means to unite with the Supreme.

Like the other great acharyas, he affirmed the Vedas as the Ultimate Truth. However, he considered the Shreemad Bhagavatam as the ripened fruit of Vedic knowledge. In particular, he was fascinated by the Chatushloki Bhagavatam. These are four verses considered as the seed of the Bhagavatam. They form a part of a dialogue at the beginning of creation between Shree Krishna and Brahma. The first of these verses defines Vallabh's philosophy.

> *aham evāsam evāgre nānyad yat sad-asat param*
> *paśhchād aham yad etach cha yo 'vaśhiṣhyeta so 'smyaham*
>
> (Bhagavatam 2.9.33)

'I alone existed prior to creation—when there were neither gross objects nor material energy. Now, all that exists is My very Form. Likewise, after annihilation, I alone will remain. There is nothing apart from Me, Shree Krishna.'

This is the viewpoint on which Vallabh founded his ideology. He proclaimed that everything is God, and named his philosophy *Brahma vada*, which propagates that Shree Krishna is the source of all creation. Both the jiva (soul) and maya are His undifferentiated energies. Thus, everything that exists is a manifestation of Shree Krishna.

Vallabh also called his school of thought *Shuddha Advait vada* (Pure Non-Dualism), sharply contrasting it with Shankaracharya's *Advaita vada* (Non-Dualism). The latter had posited that only Brahman is real and all else is false. Vallabh, in contrast, propounded that all creation is Divine. This perspective had a profound impact upon the populace because it gave people a powerful way to progress spiritually through joyous devotion.

Four-Question Challenge in Jagannath Puri

When Vallabh was only 10 years old, his father took the family on a pilgrimage to the holy city of Jagannath Puri. The visit would be a pivotal moment in the young prodigy's life, foreshadowing the future spiritual revolution he would ignite.

The ruler of Puri, King Prataprudra, had issued a challenge

that would test the mettle of the assembled scholars and acharyas. The young Vallabh was also present in their midst. The competition sought answers to four profound questions: 1) What is the greatest scripture? 2) Who is the greatest God? 3) What is the greatest mantra? 4) What is the greatest deed?

While erudite pundits grappled for a suitable answer, young Vallabh stood before the assembly. In an unwavering voice, he recited the following verse that captivated the audience:

> *eka śhāstram devakīputragītam,*
> *eko devo devakīputra eva*
> *eko mantrastasya nāmāni yāni*
> *karmāpyekam tasya devasya sevā*

'The highest scripture is Shree Krishna's words, the Bhagavad Gita. Lord Krishna is the Supreme God; the greatest mantra is His Name. And serving Him is the highest duty.' This shloka remains famous even today for its simple and powerful portrayal of *ananya bhakti* (exclusive devotion) towards one's *Iṣhṭa Dev*.

The family continued their travels and arrived at the Lord Venkateshwar Temple in Tirupati. There, Laxman Bhatt breathed his last. The widowed Illammagaru decided to return to her maternal home in Vijayanagar in South India and settled there.

Vallabh Starts Travelling and Spreading the Message of Bhakti

Though only 11 years old, Vallabh was blossoming with devotion. He had a divine mission to fulfil and left his mother to spread the nectar of bhakti. Commencing with South India, he arrived at Mangalprastha. There he encountered Dhondhi, a Jain ascetic, whose philosophy emphasized austerity as the sole path to Divinity.

Jainism was a prevailing dharma of the time. Vallabh was always welcoming and tolerant of others' spiritual beliefs. But he was aflame with the desire to connect people with God. He explained that while austerity is undeniably praiseworthy, it is not enough to attain God. Communion with the Divine requires surrender at Shree Krishna's lotus feet, and this is best achieved by immersing ourselves in loving devotion.

Next, Vallabh visited Tirupati. There, he met Ravikant, a renowned scholar who had heard of Vallabh's extraordinary genius. Intrigued by his reputation, Ravikant asked him to recite certain mantras. Vallabh not only chanted them flawlessly but also did it in the reverse order!

With each encounter, Vallabh demonstrated profound mastery of the shastras. However, he was not merely an acharya but also a spiritual alchemist, transforming rigid doctrines into blissful devotion. His goal was to inundate people with love for Shree Krishna. The gift he was offering to his followers was something beyond salvation—the ambrosia of divine prem.

Earning the Title of Vallabhacharya

From Tirupati, Vallabh journeyed to Hampi, capital of the Vijayanagar empire. Under the reign of King Krishnadevaraya, Hampi had become a famed seat of learning. On this occasion, the king had announced a grand *shastrarth* (scriptural debate). Prominent followers of Shankaracharya, Ramanujacharya, and

Madhvacharya traditions had assembled to participate.

Though just 11 years old, Vallabh courageously took the stage to present his ideology. He quoted the *Ishopanishad*:

īśhāvāsyam idam sarvam yat kiñcha jagatyām jagat

(mantra 1)

'The entire universe, with all its living and non-living beings, is the manifestation of the Supreme Being, Who dwells within it.' Hence, the Divine pervades everything in this world.

Vallabh went on to explain that the jiva is engulfed in ignorance and entangled in worldly attachments. When the soul changes its outlook and becomes God-centered, its ignorance is dispelled. By connecting with the Supreme, it too becomes *Brahma swaroop* or God-like. It then perceives the Lord everywhere and in everything. Liken this to impure water that is offered to the all-pure Ganga. It no longer remains impure; on the contrary, it becomes holy. The Ganga manifests as the goddess Ganga, the river Ganga, and the water in the Ganga. Likewise, God manifests in His personal Form as the jivas and as the world.

In this manner, Vallabh established his philosophy of *Brahma vada*, or 'everything is Krishna'. The king and the entire assembly were impressed by his clarity and profound wisdom. They applauded the young prodigy and declared him the winner. Vallabh was now given the prestigious title of Acharya, proclaiming him as *Vallabhacharya*.

To honour this conquest, King Krishnadevaraya presented the young Master with numerous gold coins and riches. But he rejected them all, keeping only seven coins for his Bhagavad pooja.

Vyas Teerth, the Guru of the Madhva Sampradaya, wished for Vallabhacharya to stay back and become his successor. But the Acharya respectfully declined. He preferred not to be confined to one place and, instead, travel across India to spread the path of bhakti.

Reverence for Everything as God

Vallabhacharya's pilgrimage led him to Vishnu Kanchi. Again, his principles and beliefs were illustrated through a profound incident at the shrine of Varadaraj Perumal, a form of Lord Vishnu. On the steps leading up to the temple, verses from Jayadeva Goswami's *Geet Govind* were inscribed. Vallabhacharya refused to climb the stairs, declaring that the composition is connected to Shree Krishna, and thus an embodiment of the Divine. Hearing such wisdom, the priests were moved and guided the Acharya through an alternate path.

In that moment, Vallabhacharya elevated the concept of *Advaita* to new heights. His refusal to climb was not a denial of non-dualism but its ultimate affirmation—that all is Brahman when you connect your consciousness with God. Through devotion, the mundane becomes Divine when you offer it to the Lord.

From this sacred encounter, Vallabhacharya journeyed to Padma Teerth, where a different kind of transformation awaited. The queen was possessed by a spirit. Seeking help, the king implored Vallabhacharya to exorcise the spirit. Shree Vallabh instructed his disciples to sprinkle sacred dust from Vrindavan upon the afflicted queen. As the holy particles settled on her, the spirit fled.

Vallabhacharya explained, 'These spirits, though they may seem mighty, are but mere specks before the radiance of Shree Krishna. What is there to fear in His shelter?' He urged all present to deepen their faith that the divine power of Krishna far surpasses any malevolent forces.

From there, his journey led him to Kumarpada, where he encountered a *kapalika* yogi, a tantric practitioner. The Tantric tradition has higher and lower paths, with some lower tantrics invoking spirits to perform minor miracles. This particular yogi boasted of his ability to control the movements of the sun and moon.

'You who claim to move the sun and moon,' Vallabh challenged, 'can you even rise from your seat without the grace of God?' The yogi tried but found himself inexplicably bound to his seat. He panicked and questioned, 'What have you done to my shakti (energies)?'

Vallabhacharya's response was as simple as it was insightful: 'I have merely uttered the name of God. There is no power greater than Him, and no force more potent than His Name.' His message was not to fear ghosts and spirits but to cultivate faith in God's protection. Doing this would not only drive away dark beings but also destroy the dark vestiges in our heart.

The cornerstone of Vallabhacharya's teachings was complete surrender to Shree Krishna. To train his followers along these lines, he taught the *Brahma Sambandh* mantra, 'Shree Krishna sharnam mama'.

Shree Vallabh explained that the *Brahma Sambandh* mantra was a heartfelt prayer: 'O Shree Krishna, in my forgetfulness of

You, I am drowning in this ocean of maya. All my efforts have failed without any means of my own to reach You. My faith now rests solely at Your lotus feet. I come seeking shelter in You.'

Through this mantra, Vallabhacharya inspired his devotees to cultivate a deep longing for God. He taught that *virah* (yearning) creates a divine pain that must be endured as austerity. The longing for God, when tolerated, purifies the heart and brings one closer to the Divine.

Darshan of Yamuna Devi

Vallabhacharya eventually reached the sacred land of Vrindavan. It was his custom to conduct *Bhagavat Saptahs*, week-long discourses on the Shreemad Bhagavatam, wherever he went. The sacred land of Shree Krishna drew scores of listeners, from near and far, for his dissertations.

His pilgrimage then led him to Gokul, where Shree Krishna had spent His first two years. There, he sought to identify Thakurani Ghat and Govind Ghat, along the Yamuna River. According to legend, the goddess Yamuna appeared before him, saying, 'Acharya, this is Thakurani Ghat, and that is Govind Ghat.'

Vallabh felt blessed to have darshan of Mother Yamuna. With reverence and gratitude, he composed the *Yamuna Ashtakam*. His devotional raptures towards Mother Yamuna can be glimpsed in this translation of its first verse:

'I joyfully bow to Shree Yamunaji, the bestower of divine energy. Her sprawling sands gleam radiantly like the lotus feet of Shree Krishna. The fragrance of flowers from lush forests along her banks mingles with her waters, making her aromatic. Both humble and assertive gopis worship Yamunaji, recognizing that she embodies the splendour of Shree Krishna.'

In the *Yamuna Ashtakam*, Vallabh perceives Shree Krishna's presence and glory in every aspect of the sacred river. In the end, he boldly declared that chanting the *Yamuna Ashtakam* would result in love at the lotus feet of his Beloved Lord. Accordingly, this composition became an important part of his teachings and an integral aspect of his worship.

Journey to Govardhan

Vallabhacharya continued his travels and eventually reached Jharkhand. There, he received a divine call from Shree Krishna: 'Return to Braj. I am waiting for you at Govardhan in the form of Govardhan Nathji.'

The deity of Govardhan Nathji is known today as Shrinathji. It is enshrined at Nathdwara in Rajasthan and is the presiding deity of the followers of Pushti Marg.

When Vallabhacharya arrived at Govardhan, he discovered the priest tending to Govardhan Nathji was doing a shoddy job. Shree Vallabh took charge and placed the deity in a more sanctified position. He then sought out sincere devotees for the pooja and taught them the proper art of service.

Vallabh's passion for Govardhan Nathji was exceedingly contagious. It ignited fervour among the villagers to participate in the worship of the Lord. Every day, they would lovingly serve Nathji with milk, curd, and other edibles. With the most beautiful clothes, they would dress the deity and meticulously ornament Him with precious jewels.

In a few months, Shrinathji became the heart and soul of the villagers. They celebrated festivals and worshipped Him with great enthusiasm. On one occasion, Nathji expressed to the Acharya the desire for a cow. Vallabh conveyed the request to the villagers, who lovingly began gifting cows to the Deity. Soon, Shrinathji's herd grew into thousands, leading to the creation of a *goshala* (cowshed).

Subsequently, a large temple was built for Shrinathji. Vallabhacharya predicted that the prominent temple would draw the attention of invaders. He foresaw that Nathji would eventually move westward to Nathdwara in Rajasthan—a prophecy that would later come true.

Once, a devotee came for darshan of Vallabhacharya at the Shrinathji Temple. He was carrying his *Thakur Batwa*, a small bag to hold his Beloved Laddu Gopal deity. In his eagerness to meet his Gurudev, he carelessly hung the bag somewhere within the temple precincts. The devotee attended Shree Vallabh's satsang and then took leave of his Guru. As he prepared to depart, he realized he had forgotten where he placed his *Thakur Batwa*. He approached his Guru with a sense of embarrassment and sought guidance.

The acharya gently but firmly admonished him, saying, 'Is this how you show attentiveness to your God? If you truly believe He is divine, then why such carelessness? Is that your devotion? When we perform seva for the Lord, it should be done with utmost care and attention. This care is an expression of love.'

Through this gentle reprimand, Vallabhacharya conveyed that genuine devotion requires vigilance and respect.

Teaching Worship of God as a Child

Vallabhacharya then journeyed to Gujarat, which became the main centre of his spiritual work. He introduced a simple and natural form of bhakti to the people. He taught the people of Gujarat *vatsalya bhav*—a loving, parental approach to worship. Vallabh instructed devotees to build havelis (temples) and worship Shree Krishna as their Bal-Gopal. These havelis would be safe havens for baby Krishna—temples where He would be protected, cherished, and loved to the utmost. He encouraged attending to the little One with a sense of responsibility and tender care of a parent.

Devotees embraced and readily adopted the parental bhav. To that effect, they would not perform morning aarti too early, as their darling Krishna was a little child who needed His rest. Similarly, they would put their Baby to bed early at night since infants need more sleep. This practice continues to this day, with evening prayers in Pushti Marg temples ending early to allow the Deity to rest.

The havelis established by the followers of Vallabhacharya exude warmth and simplicity. They beautifully reflect the natural, playful devotion he encouraged.

Inspiration from the Gopis

Vallabhacharya then made his way to Gopi Talab, a serene pond about 25 kilometres from Dwarika in Gujarat. He was again challenged by followers of other sects ready to engage in discussions. However, they all became faithful devotees when he touched their hearts with sublime thoughts and wisdom.

At Gopi Talab, he shared a beautiful Leela illustrating the unwavering devotion of the gopis of Braj.

During Krishna's time in Dwarika, Rukmini and Satyabhama, his queens, questioned him about the Maharaas. Shree Krishna had played His flute and called the gopis but not His 16,108 future queens. 'Why did you not call any of us?' they asked with curiosity.

Shree Krishna smiled and cautioned them, 'The gopis renounced all worldly attachments for Me. You would not be able to make the sacrifices that they made.'

To demonstrate this, Krishna decided to put their devotion to the test. He played his flute at Gopi Talab, and the enchanting sound reached the gopis in Vrindavan. They instantly abandoned everything at the call of their Beloved and ran all the way to the lake.

In contrast, the queens of Dwarika also heard Shree Krishna's flute, but they found themselves entangled in worldly concerns. 'My son's school is about to open,' one said. 'What will my father-in-law say?' another pondered. Their worldly attachments held them back. As a result, only five queens made it to the talab.

Vallabhacharya took the opportunity to highlight the gopis' matchless dedication and complete surrender to Shree Krishna. They only desired to selflessly serve their Beloved for His pleasure. This made them fearless and indifferent to disrepute. Hence, they forsook all worldly attachments for Him and arrived at the lake in response to their Divine Beloved.

Such all-consuming devotion of the gopis is the idyllic standard for seekers of divine love. Sage Narad, a bhakti saint of the highest order, exalts these simple village maidens. He declares them 'the greatest acharyas of bhakti'. He states in the *Narad Bhakti Darshan*:

yathā vrajagopikānām   (sutra 21)

Narad Muni explains that devotion for Shree Krishna should be like the gopis of Vrindavan. Such love is imbued with sacrifice, selflessness, and tolerance. It binds the Almighty—He who is ever free gets defeated by selfless pure love!

Marriage and Subsequent Sanyas

After his travels, Vallabhacharya arrived in Pandharpur. There, he received a divine message from Pandharinath (Vitthal) Bhagavan, 'You live amongst householders. To truly understand and guide them, you must become one of them. Embrace the life of a grihasta (householder), and let your example serve as an ideal for others.' Heeding this directive, Vallabh got married and had two children.

At this point, he embarked on his third great yatra, revisiting many sacred places. Mahaprabhu Vallabhacharya was now on the last leg of his third yatra. He arrived in Braj, where he established eight prominent disciples known as *aṣhṭachāp sakhās*. These were eight great poet-saints who resided in the holy land and wrote bhajans on the Leelas of Shree Krishna. Soordas was Vallabh's most distinguished and renowned protégé.

At the age of 52, Vallabhacharya embraced sanyas and moved to Prayag to spend the last part of his life. There, he dedicated himself to writing various shastras to guide souls on the path of bhakti. Among his notable works are the *Subodhini*, a commentary on the Shreemad Bhagavatam, and the *Anubhashya*, a commentary on the *Brahma Sutras*, along with many other sacred texts.

The Acharya's stay in Prayag had its pain points. The scholars there often engaged him in relentless debates. Finally, he left for a more solitary place called Adel, where he remained till the end of his life. He completed his scholarly works, contributing significantly to devotional literature.

Particularly famous amongst Vallabhacharya's works are his *Ashtakams*, compositions in eight stanzas. The *Nandkumar Ashtakam's* verses enchant the mind with Krishna's divine beauty while also alluding to His charming Pastimes. Here is the translation of the first verse:

'Salutations to Shree Nandakumar, the enchanting Gopal of Vrindavan, adorned with a *vanamala* (garland) that graces His chest. He captivates all with His large, expressive eyes. His very presence alleviates the sufferings of His devotees. He is the bright moon of Vrindavan and a source of enormous joy. Embodying supreme bliss, He holds the earth within Him. He is the Beloved Ghanashyam, Who is self-content in His divine nature. He is immensely pleasurable and rouses love in everyone. Worship this essence of all joy, Nandakumar, by contemplating His divine nature—He is the Supreme Brahman.'

Vallabhacharya's most famous and exquisite devotional hymn is the *Madhurashtakam*. In it, Shree Krishna is depicted as the epitome of sweetness. Some of its famous verses are shared here:

adharam madhuram vadanam madhuram
nayanam madhuram hasitam madhuram
hridayam madhuram gamanam madhuram
madhurādhipaterakhilam madhuram ||1||

'His lips are sweet, His face is sweet, His eyes are sweet, His smile is sweet. His heart is sweet, His gait (walk) is sweet. Everything is absolutely sweet about the Lord of Sweetness.'

veṇurmadhuro reṇurmadhuraḥ
pāṇirmadhuraḥ pādau madhurau
nṛityam madhuram sakhyam madhuram
madhurādhipaterakhilam madhuram ||3||

'His flute is sweet, His foot-dust is sweet, His hands are sweet, His feet are sweet. His dancing is sweet, His friendship is sweet. Everything is absolutely sweet about the Lord of Sweetness.'

gopi madhurā līlā madhurā
yuktam madhuram muktam madhuram
dṛishṭam madhuram śhishṭam madhuram
madhurādhipaterakhilam madhuram ||7||

'His gopis are sweet, His Pastimes are sweet, His union is sweet, His deliverance is sweet. His sidelong glances are sweet, His etiquette is sweet. Everything is absolutely sweet about the Lord of Sweetness.'

The composition serves as a guide for devotees of the Pushti Marg, prompting them to remain in a constant love-laden state of Krishna. It ignites longing in the soul for union with God, propelling it towards realization of the Divine.

Through his life and teachings, Vallabhacharya left an indelible mark on the spiritual landscape of India. His prominence as an elevated bhakti saint was no less than that of a Jagadguru. He guided countless souls towards a deeper connection with their Beloved Lord, through loving service and remembrance. Even today, his legacy continues to inspire, offering a path where reverence and devotion transform the ordinary into the Divine.

11

Tyagaraja

Tyagaraja was an eighteenth-century saint from South India, admired worldwide for his devotional compositions in Carnatic music. True to his name, 'the king of renunciation', Tyaga-raja exemplified utmost detachment, though living a family life.

From childhood itself, Tyagaraja was enraptured by the Pastimes of Lord Ram. Listening to them, love for Bhagavan Ram became deeply rooted in his heart. His unwavering devotion combined with God-given musical talent shaped his life's journey and accomplishments. He regarded music as a way of experiencing God's love and effortlessly composed thousands of devotional hymns, starting at the young age of eight years.

Tyagaraja pursued music solely with devotional intent, without focusing on the technical intricacies of classical music. In doing so, he paid attention to his bhav, instead of the actual theories, intricacies, and technicalities required. And yet, he revolutionized Indian music with the brilliant innovativeness of a creative genius. His trademark style was the *Pancharatna Kritis*. Each *kriti* included five songs, all set in different talas and ragas. The dignity, devotional splendour, and literary beauty of these compositions remain unparalleled. They are perceived as mystical by novices and seasoned musicians alike.

Tyagaraja attracted widespread fame in his lifetime itself. People from all walks of life thronged to meet and honour him. This included the artists and the ordinary; the royalty and commoners; the rich and the poor; and the devout and the atheists. He is considered one of the three giants of Carnatic music, along with Shyama Shastri and Muthuswamy Dikshitar.

Tyagaraja is also revered as one of the three famous Telugu *vāggeyakārs*—composers who also crafted ragas and performed them. The two other *vāggeyakārs* were the Saints Annamacharya and Ramadasu.

The Seeds of Devotion in Infancy

Tyagaraja was born on 4 May 1767 to a Telugu family in a city called Thiruvarur, nestled in the district of Thanjavur, Tamil Nadu. His father, Rama Brahmam, was a highly respected scholar known for his enchanting discourses on the Ramayan.

Tyagaraja's birth was foretold by the presiding Deity of Thiruvarur. The Lord informed Rama Brahmam that his third son would be a noble soul and should be named *Tyagaraja*, meaning 'king of renunciation'. Unlike his first two sons, who were incompetent and dissipated, the coming child would be a beacon of talent and virtue. Inspired by this holy revelation, Rama Brahmam ensured that Tyagaraja received proper education in Sanskrit, Telugu, and astrology.

His parents observed that as an infant, Tyagaraja would stop breastfeeding on hearing music. So, his mother, a virtuoso in the compositions of Purandara Dasa, nurtured his musical prowess. The knowledge he imbibed during childhood enabled him to compose varieties of ragas in later years.

Since childhood, sanyasis played a prominent role in Tyagaraja's life. Once, at the tender age of five, he was so sick that his father feared losing him. However, a sanyasi appeared mysteriously and comforted Rama Brahmam saying that Tyagaraja would soon recover and achieve great heights in life. Remarkably, Tyagaraja recovered completely the next day itself.

Subsequently also, whenever Tyagaraja encountered challenges in life and needed guidance, divine interventions illuminated his path towards light and triumph.

The Musical Prodigy

Since his father was a narrator of the Ramayan, Tyagaraja got the opportunity to hear about the Pastimes of Bhagavan Ram from infancy. The episodes captivated his heart, and he often dreamt of Ram. He would spend hours immersed in visualising Ram's Leelas. Concurrently, he grew uninterested in worldly pursuits and shunned mundane talks. There was no temple of Shree Ram nearby, but Tyagaraja's father worshipped images of Ram, Sita, and Lakshman in his home. He initiated his son into the same devotional practice.

As a child, Tyagaraja would pluck flowers from a neighbour's garden for his father's pooja. Near the garden was the home of Sonti Venkataramanayya, a famous music teacher, who ran his own school. On his way back, Tyagaraja would listen to the music lessons imparted by the teacher to his students. One day Rama Brahmam observed his son listening with rapt attention.

He requested Sonti Venkataramanayya to teach music to his son. The guru agreed and soon discovered the tremendous musical talent his pupil possessed.

From his teacher, Tyagaraja quickly learned music and the veena in a short span of one and a half years. He was now well-versed in classical Carnatic music. Its symphony further sweetened the devotional sentiments pervading his heart.

Bhagavan Ram's Darshan

Tyagaraja married at the age of 18. Soon after, his father passed away. Now Tyagaraja and his wife lived with his eldest brother, Jalapesan. The brother, motivated by greed, saw potential profit from Tyagaraja's musical talents. Jalapesan asked him to teach music to the devadasis—women who danced in the temple.

In ancient times, the devadasis were devout, considering the temple Deity as their husband and dedicating their lives to worship. But, with the progress of Kaliyug, they had fallen into ill repute. Thus, the saintly Tyagaraja refused to teach music to these dancers in adherence to his ethics.

Jalapesan was furious at his younger brother's denial. He retaliated by throwing Tyagaraja's deity of Shree Ram in the Kaveri River. When Tyagaraja returned home to discover his Beloved Deity missing, he was heartbroken. He wept continuously in separation from his Lord and lost interest in life. His anguish found expression in the mournful song, *Endu dagi nado*, in which he states:

'O Ram, why do You hide yourself? Please listen to my appeal. When Hiranyakashipu oppressed his son greatly, Bhagavan could not tolerate and manifested from a pillar. When Bali thrashed his brother Sugreev, the Lord protected him from behind a palm tree.

Similarly, You must be hiding so that You can destroy my wicked deeds from past lives, annihilate the internal enemies of desire, anger, and greed, and protect Your faithful devotees, including Tyagaraja. Who knows where You are hiding today and when will You have the compassion to reveal Yourself?'

Three months later, Tyagaraja had a dream revealing the precise location of the Deity on the bed of the Kaveri River. He rushed to the spot and retrieved his Beloved Lord. With infinite joy, he brought the Deity back home.

A while later, the two brothers fought again, and Jalapesan threw Tyagaraja and his wife out of the house. The ousted couple spent the entire day on the streets until the local tahsildar was petitioned by well-wishers to settle the matter. The tahsildar got the house partitioned into two, allotting half to each brother. Finally, by nightfall, Tyagaraja and his wife had a roof over their heads.

Soon an enchanting couple arrived at their door, accompanied by a dutiful servant. The couple introduced themselves as travellers and requested food. Tyagaraja had just entered his new home and had nothing to offer. He felt extremely embarrassed at not being able to provide hospitality to the visitors. Seeing his discomfort, the gentleman affectionately addressed him, 'Tyagu! Do not worry. We are carrying provisions, and our servant will take care of the cooking.'

Tyagaraja was surprised at the stranger's affectionate address.

Shortly after, they all greatly enjoyed the dinner. The night passed in animated conversation, and the couple left the next morning. Only after they had gone, Tyagaraja got the sudden revelation, 'O My God! These visitors were none other than Bhagavan Ram, Sita, and Hanuman.' He instantly sang a *kriti*, *Bhav anuta* in Mohan raga, in which he expressed his bittersweet realization, 'O Lord, Who came to my house without even letting me know. You spoke to me so lovingly and intimately. You must be tired. Why did You leave? Please rest in my heart and free Yourself of Your weariness'.

From that day on, with the blessings of Prabhu Ram, Tyagaraja's compositions acquired a cosmic touch. He wrote soulful bhajans glorifying Shree Ram's Names, Forms, Leelas, and Virtues.

Once Haridas, a sadhu from Kanchipuram, met Tyagaraja in Tiruvaiyaru. He ardently proclaimed that any devotee who chants Ram Naam 96 crore times will get darshan of Shree Ram. Tyagaraja embraced this as a divine command. He resolved to chant the Name of Ram 125,000 times every day. His wife became his partner, and together, they completed the number of 96 crore chants in 21 years.

On fulfilling the tally, Tyagaraja eagerly waited for a vision of Shree Ram that would truly satisfy his heart. As months passed without darshan, his anticipation turned into deep sorrow. In longing for his Beloved Lord, he wandered in deep lamentation and sang the famous *kriti*, titled *Marugelaraa*:

marugelarā? o rāghava!

'O Raghav! Why have You placed a veil between You and me?'

> *marugela charāchararūpa! parātparā*
> *sūryasudhākaralochana!*

'Why are You hiding, O Lord of both moving and non-moving beings? O Supreme Who is beyond everything. O Lord Who has the Sun and Moon as His eyes. O Raghava! Why this shield between us?'

> *anni nīvanuchu nantarangamuna*
> *dinnagā vedaki telisikonṭinayya*

'Having searched deeply in my heart, I have directly perceived and realized that You alone pervade everything.'

> *ninnegāni madi nennajāla norula*
> *nannu brovavayyā, tyāgarājanuta*

'I vow never to let my mind dwell on anyone but You. O Lord, Tyagaraja offers his heartfelt prayers to You! Please protect me and bestow darshan.'

As Tyagaraja completed his beseeching and soulful bhajan, Bhagavan Ram revealed Himself in His divine form. Tyagaraja was ecstatic that his devotion of 21 years had been accepted.

Living Up to the Meaning of His Name

Tyagaraja embodied the spirit of his name and was veritably a paragon of renunciation. At the core of his nature was utmost indifference to worldly assets.

A wealthy businessman of Chennai, Sundara Mudaliyar, was an ardent admirer of the great composer. He wished to express appreciation by offering gifts but knew very well that Tyagaraja would not accept anything. Once, when the Saint was returning from Chennai to Thiruvaiyaru, Sundar Mudaliyar secretly placed a bag with 1000 gold coins in his cart. He convinced Tyagaraja's disciples to utilize the sum for celebrating Ram Navami and other festivals. They agreed, considering the spiritual intention behind the gift.

During the journey, Tyagaraja and disciples reached Nagalapuram, a village notorious for bandits. These goons would inflict injuries on passersby with pebbles shot from catapults. After the travellers surrendered, they would be looted.

Soon enough, the robbers surrounded the Saint's procession. Panicking, the disciples whispered into Tyagaraja's ears about the thieves. He responded, 'What do we have to fear? We have no valuables for them to steal.'

The disciples confessed about the gold. Upon learning of the wealth in his cart, Tyagaraja instructed his disciples to hand over all the gold to the thieves. A disciple objected, 'It was a gift to be used for celebrating festivals. We must take care of it for Bhagavan Ram's sake.'

Tyagaraja parried him, 'If it is God's money, let Him take care of it.'

Saying this, he sat down in meditation, and began singing, *Mundu venaka iru*, meaning: 'O Ram, The slayer of Mura and Khara! Come, come quickly with Lakshman to protect me and rescue Your property.'

Miraculously, two valiant young men on horseback appeared on the scene; they rained arrows at the robbers and chased them away. Freed from the menace, Tyagaraja and his troupe continued their journey.

The thieves, though foiled, were curious to know about the heroic men who had appeared out of the blue. They followed the procession. When it halted, they reverentially approached Tyagaraja and inquired about the two heroes. Inferring it as divine intervention, Tyagaraja composed the *kriti, Enta bhagyamo* in Sarang raga. In this bhajan, Tyagaraja conveys his gratitude and immense fortune of being personally cared for by the Supreme Lord Himself. The One who is matchless has affectionately comforted his heart, erased all his worries, and shielded him just as He protected the revered Sages who came before.

Transformed by this experience, the thieves abandoned their immoral ways and turned over a new leaf. Tyagaraja instructed them to chant Ram Naam and loot the eternal treasure of bhakti that would not hurt anyone.

A Life Exclusively Dedicated to God

The local king of the region was Raja Sarabhoji. Profuse admiration for Tyagaraja's exceptional compositions had reached his ears. Impressed by the acclaim of many, the king desired to hear the musician himself. He sent two officials to inform Tyagaraja to prepare a composition glorifying the king. The Saint would then receive the honour of performing it at the court. In return, he would be rewarded with land, wealth, and numerous other treasures.

As a child, Tyagaraja had accompanied his father to the king's palace for Ram kathas. But he was now indignant at the royal request. He was being summoned to use his God-given talents in praise of a mere mortal.

In response, Tyagaraja composed an impromptu piece titled *Nidhi chala sukhama*. The song is a series of rhetorical questions addressed to his mind.

> *nidhi chāla sukhamā? rāmuni sannidhi seva sukhamā, nijamuga balku manasā!*

'O mind, tell the truth. Are worldly treasures more gratifying than the bliss of the Lord Himself?'

> *dadhi navanīta kṣhīramulu ruchiyo? dāśharathi dhyāna bhajana sudhārasamu ruchiyo?*

'O mind, if you want to relish something, partake the nectar of Ram's remembrances and devotion. Why seek the king's offering of milk, butter, and yoghurt?'

> *mamata bandhana yuta narastuti sukhamā? sumati tyāgarājanutuni kīrtana sukhamā?*

'O mind, sing the glories of the Bhagavan, Whom Tyagaraja has praised. Do not flatter mere men who are trapped by their own petty ego.'

A beautiful lesson we can learn from this is about Tyagaraja's perspective towards his extraordinary talent. He was untouched by pride, attributing his abilities to divine grace. He firmly believed Bhagavan Ram had gifted him with musical brilliance, and he saw himself as the caretaker of the craft. Thus, he was firmly convinced that all his poetic and musical skills should be dedicated to glorifying the Supreme.

Tyagaraja set a blazing example that spirituality does not require us to renounce our talents. Rather, we must use them to do our works as an offering to the Lord. Thus, every form of art—dance, music, architecture, or literature—can serve the

Supreme Source. In fact, historically, the finest litterateurs, composers, architects, and poets have often been saintly devotees.

Tyagaraja's outright rejection of royal patronage highlighted his purity of intent. However, the palace officials were unprepared for such a rebuff. They conveyed Tyagaraja's response to the king, who was highly annoyed. His big ego had been punctured by a mere poet. With his vanity hurt, he sent soldiers to kill Tyagaraja and fetch his dead body.

However, as soon as these soldiers left the palace, the king was seized by a severe stomach ache. None of the royal physicians could alleviate it. Then, an astrologer opined that this ailment was the consequence of insulting a noble soul. Coming to his senses, Sarabhoji immediately sent another set of soldiers to rescind his previous order. Thereafter, the king himself proceeded to meet Tyagaraja. He bowed down at the Saint's feet and begged forgiveness for his mistake. Subsequently, the king and Tyagaraja became good friends.

Tyagaraja Visits Tirupati

In 1839, Tyagaraja embarked on a pilgrimage to the Land of the Seven Hills, Tirupati. In those days, there was no proper road to the temple hilltop, so pilgrims had to walk 12 kilometres through the forest path that was teeming with tigers and other wild animals.

By the time Tyagaraja and his disciples reached the temple, it was past noon. Leaving the disciples to bathe, the eager Tyagaraja rushed straight to the Deity for darshan but found that the curtain was closed for the afternoon as the Deities were resting. Deprived of the darshan of Lord Venkateshwara, Tyagaraja began to sob like a child. His feelings spontaneously crystallized into a melodious kirtan, dedicated to Bhagavan Venkatesh.

> tera tīyaga rādā loni,
> tiruppati venkaṭaramaṇa matsaramu

'O Tirupati Venkataramana! Will You not remove the inner veil of anger, arrogance, and jealousy that has deeply rooted itself within me?'

Tyagaraja's humility shines forth in this composition. He perceives the curtain hiding the Divine from his sight as a symbol of his own pride. Hence, he prays for divine grace, which alone can lift the veil of ignorance, allowing him to see God in all His glory.

The kirtan was so emotionally surcharged that it melted God's heart. As soon as Tyagaraja concluded his imploring, the curtain miraculously fell asunder, revealing Lord Venkateshwara. Tyagaraja thanked the Lord, with tears streaming down his face and a choked voice. In his deep, ecstatic experience, he sang *Venkatesa ninnu*, expressing, 'One needs 10,000 eyes to behold You, O Lord Venkateshwara!'

Tyagaraja's enchanting devotional singing drew devotees in large numbers, and they all witnessed this miracle. The temple acharyas were also left speechless on witnessing Bhagavan Venkatesh's way of honouring the great composer.

A powerful takeaway from this episode is the deep longing for God in Saints, which is the essence of bhakti. Tyagaraja's desire for 10,000 eyes reminds us of King Prithu in the Shreemad Bhagavatam. Bhagavan Vishnu gave him darshan and told him to ask for a boon. Prithu responded with the most amazing request:

> na kāmaye nātha tad apy aham kvacin
> na yatra yuṣmac-caraṇāmbujāsavaḥ
> mahattamāntar-hṛdayān mukha-cyuto
> vidhatsva karṇāyutam eṣa me varaḥ   (4.20.24)

In this verse, Prithu rejects both aspirations for bhukti (worldly joys) and mukti (liberation). Instead, he prays for ten thousand ears to relish the sweet Pastimes of God.

Similarly, we hear of the longing of the gopis for Shree Krishna. In the land of Braj, every evening, the gopis would await Gopal's return from grazing the cows. When they would finally see their Divine Beloved, they would complain to Brahma that his design of the human body was faulty. He had given them only two eyes, and even these had eyelids that interrupted the vision while blinking. Did Brahma not realize that this would hinder their sight to behold their Beloved Krishna?

Such deep yearning for God forms the very core of bhakti. Saints have stated it in various ways. Sage Narad called it *param vyākulatā*, or supreme longing. Shankaracharya referred to it as *mumukṣhutv*, meaning the intense thirst for salvation. Ramanujacharya termed it *tāp*, or devotional austerity. Vallabhacharya called it *sādhan hīnatā*, or deep cry for God's grace. Nimbarkacharya referred to it as *niḥśhreyas*, or the most auspicious emotion. Tyagaraja expressed the same emotion in his *Venkatesa ninnu* bhajan.

Living In Adherence to the Will of God

Despite being a householder with a family, Tyagaraja led an austere life. He considered it sufficient to have a hut for shelter. With complete disregard for worldly comforts, he refused to earn a livelihood. For food, he would subsist on alms, collecting only what he needed for the day. It was a hand-to-mouth existence, while his mind soared high, scaling sublime levels of devotion. He was a true ideal of 'Simple living, high thinking'.

Tyagaraja did not sing for money or fame. Music to him was not merely an art, but a sacred practice of worshipping God. Blending music and devotion, Tyagaraja taught the *Gaana Marg* of reciting the Lord's Names. His music became a medium for evoking devotional thoughts en masse in the wider populace.

Tyagaraja presented the profound truths of the Upanishads in a simple, accessible manner. Harnessing metaphors and similes from daily life, he made complex philosophical concepts easily comprehensible. For this reason, his repository is sometimes called *Tyaga Brahmopanishad*.

Although Tyagaraja did not believe in testing his faith or performing miracles, a few widely known exceptions exist. Once, while crossing a temple in Puttur, he encountered a group of people surrounding a dead man, with a grieving lady and child beside him. Tyagaraja learned they were pilgrims and had arrived at the temple the previous night. They had wanted to take shelter in the temple courtyard. In an attempt to open the locked doors, the man tried to scale the wall in the dark. Unfortunately, he had fallen into a well on the other side and drowned. His dead body was discovered the next morning.

Moved by their plight, Tyagaraja prayed to Shree Ram in his signature style through a *kriti*. God responded to his entreaty, and the husband miraculously regained his life-airs. Apart from a few such episodes, Tyagaraja shunned miracles, and like most Saints, chose not to display supernatural feats.

Creating a Cradle for Indian Music

Saint Tyagaraja's compositions employ a variety of tones—invoking, entreating, praising, and even scolding Lord Ram. His compositions are a blend of sublime music and splendid literature, both rooted in bhakti.

Typically, Tyagaraja would experience moments of divine inspiration, during which compositions readily flowed from his heart and tongue as he sat before the deity of Lord Ram. His *kritis* were usually structured in three major sections: *Pallavi*, *Anupallavi*, and *Charan*. This structure allowed him to introduce the theme, further develop it, and eventually amplify it with an elucidation extolling the Lord's Names, Forms, Virtues, and Pastimes. His disciples recorded his compositions on palm leaves. One disciple concentrated on the *Pallavi*, noting it carefully, then went to the nearby river to memorize it. The second focused on the *Anupallavi* and left for another place to learn it. The third noted the *Charan* and also sought solitude to memorize it. The fourth disciple wrote the pure *sahitya* (poetry) after comprehending it. The next day, the disciples would gather to consolidate their notes and present them to their Master.

Tyagaraja skilfully composed in all 72 Mela ragas. It is said that he composed nearly 24,000 songs, however, he did not systematically organize them. Hence, a significant number are lost, with only 700 *kritis* available today.

In addition to *kritis*, Tyagaraja composed two musical plays: *Prahalad Bhakti Vijayam* and *Nauka Charitam*. *Prahalad Bhakti Vijayam* consists of five acts with 45 *kritis* encompassing 138 verses, which have been set in 28 ragas, in different metres in Telugu. In it, he also pays tribute to Purandara Dasa whom he had accepted as his *manasic* Guru. *Nauka Charitam* is the most popular opera composed by Tyagaraja. It is a short Telugu play in one act with 21 *kritis* encompassing 43 verses set in 13 ragas. Tyagaraja also composed several simple devotional bhajans.

An interesting aspect of his compositions is that even while narrating the Pastimes of other Avatars, he attributes them to Shree Ram. For example, in the *Prahalad Bhakti Vijayam*, he says that Bhagavan Ram descended to rescue Prahalad. The great Saint was not unaware of the fact that Lord Ram descended after Bhagavan Narsingh. However, in his exclusive devotion to Shree Ram, Tyagaraja perceived only Ram in all Forms.

In one of his last compositions, *Kshinamai tiruga*, written shortly before his disappearance from the world, he gave a parting message to humanity. In it, he asserts that true everlasting bliss is found exclusively in the bhajan of Shree Ram. All else—including yajna, tapa, japa, *vrata* (fasting), pooja—merely lead to rebirth. Through the bhajan, he reinforces the gaana yog that was his life's work.

Tyagaraja Aradhana is a commemorative music festival held annually for over a century. This week-long celebration of music in Tyagaraja's honour takes place in Thiruvaiyaru, the town where he grew up and lived. It attracts Carnatic musicians from around the globe. The highlight of the event is the rendition of Tyagaraja's *Pancharatna Kritis*, which are sung together by everyone present, thereby infusing the atmosphere with a sacred spirit. In this way, the powerful compositions continue to resonate deeply, touching the hearts of listeners even in present times.

Leaving a Legacy of Music

Tyagaraja lived for 77 years in Thiruvaiyaru and ascended to the heavenly abode on 6 January 1847. Some believe that Tyagraja was an incarnation of Sage Valmiki who descended on earth to compose kirtans of the divine pastimes illustrated in the Ramayan. Both Valmiki and Tyagaraja had composed Ramayan in 24,000 verses. The former used the *marga sangeet* format, while Tyagaraja's *kritis* were in the *deshya sangeet* format.

To glorify Bhagavan Ram and His Pastimes, Sage Valmiki was guided by the epitome of devotion, Sage Narad. Similarly, to explore the deeper aspects of Carnatic music and devotion, Tyagaraja also revered the celestial musician, Sage Narad. In return, Narad bestowed him with the musical treatise *Svararnavam*, or 'Ocean of Musical Tones'.

In one of his soul-stirring songs, *Epaniko janminchitinani*, Tyagaraja reveals the purpose of his life, 'O Ram! Are You not aware of the reason for my birth in this world? Like Valmiki and other sages who have sung Your praises, will my yearning also be fulfilled?'

Tyajaraja created literature to infuse devotion in souls, not just in his era but for generations to come. Through his ethereal compositions, Tyagaraja established that divine love is what truly matters in this world, while everything else is merely ephemeral. He gifted humankind with a limitless legacy of music that has resonated universally across time and hearts.

Glossary

ajnana	lack of knowledge, ignorance
Alvars	12 poet-saints of South India who propounded worship of Lord Vishnu
amla	Indian gooseberry
Anant Shesh	the divine serpent upon whom Lord Vishnu rests
ananya bhakti	exclusive devotion
Bhagavan	God
bhakti	devotion; love for God
bhav	devotional sentiments
Brahma Muhurt	also known as Creator's time. Approximately the last two hours of the night immediately preceding sunrise
darshan	to see/view
Ekadashi	eleventh day of waxing and waning moon
gopis	the village maidens who resided in Braj when Shree Krishna displayed His leelas there 5,000 years ago
Guru	a God-realized teacher of spirituality
Iṣhṭa Dev	chosen Form of God for worship
jiva	individual soul

Kali yug	present era on the earth planet. It was preceded by Dwapar yug, Treta yug, and Satya yug.
kirtan	hearing, singing and remembering the Names, Forms, Qualities, Pastimes, Abodes, and Associates of God; usually done in a group
Leelas	divine pastimes of God
madhurya bhav	worship of God with conjugal sentiments
mithya	illusion, non-existent
nirantar bhakti	continuous devotion
nishkām bhakti	selfless devotion
para bhakti	divine love
prem	divine love
ragas	musical notes
samadhi	state of deep meditation
sambandhi	our true and eternal relative, who is God
sampradaya	spiritual lineage that follows set practices and can be traced back to one Guru
Sanatan Dharma	Eternal Religion
sanskars	tendencies from previous lifetimes
sanyas	monkhood; renounced order of life
satsang	holy association that takes our mind to the Absolute Truth and purifies our mind
Satya yug	the first and longest of the four yugas

	(ages) based on the Indian concept of time
shakti	energy
shastrarth	scriptural debate
shastras	scriptures
Tulsi	holy basil
Vaishnavas	followers of Bhagavan Vishnu
vatsalya bhav	sentiment of paternal affection for God
virah bhav	deep yearning for God in separation
yajnas	fire sacrifice

Guide to Hindi Pronunciation

Vowels

अ	a	as *u* in 'but'
आ	ā	as *a* in 'far'
इ	i	as *i* in 'pin'
ई	ī	as *i* in 'machine'
उ	u	as *u* in 'push'
ऊ	ū	as *o* in 'move'
ए	e	as *a* in 'evade'
ऐ	ai	as *a* in 'mat'; sometimes as ai in 'aisle' with the only difference that *a* should be pronounced as *u* in 'but', not as *a* in 'far'
ओ	o	as *o* in 'go'
औ	au	as *o* in 'pot' or as *aw* in 'saw'
ऋ	ṛi	as *ri* in 'Krishna'[1]
ॠ	ṝī	as *ree* in 'spree'

---

[1] Across the many states of India, ṛi is pronounced as *ru* as *u* in 'push'. In most parts of North India, ṛi is pronounced as *ri* in 'Krishna'. We have used the North Indian style here.

Consonants

Gutturals: Pronounced from the throat

क	ka	as *k* in 'kite'
ख	kha	as *kh* in 'Eckhart'
ग	ga	as *g* in 'goat'
घ	gha	as *gh* in 'dighard'
ङ	ṅa	as *n* in 'finger'

Palatals: Pronounced with the middle of the tongue against the palate

च	cha	as *ch* in 'channel'
छ	chha	as *chh* in 'staunchheart'
ज	ja	as *j* in 'jar'
झ	jha	as *dgeh* in 'hedgehog'
ञ	ña	as *n* in 'lunch'

Cerebrals: Pronounced with the tip of the tongue against the palate

ट	ṭa	as *t* in 'tub'
ठ	ṭha	as *th* in 'hothead'
ड	ḍa	as *d* in 'divine'
ढ	ḍha	as *dh* in 'redhead'
ण	ṇa	as *n* in 'burnt'

Dentals: Pronounced like the cerebrals but with the tongue against the teeth

त	ta	as *t* in the French word 'matron'
थ	tha	as *th* in 'ether'

द	da	as *th* in 'either'
ध	dha	as *dh* in 'Buddha'
न	na	as *n* in 'no'

Labials: Pronounced with the lips

प	pa	as *p* in 'pink'
फ	pha	as *ph* in 'uphill'
ब	ba	as *b* in 'boy'
भ	bha	as *bh* in 'abhor'
म	ma	as *m* in 'man'

Semi-vowels

य	ya	as *y* in 'yes'
र	ra	as *r* in 'remember'
ल	la	as *l* in 'light'
व	va	as *v* in 'vine', as *w* in 'swan'

Sibilants

श	śha	as *sh* in 'shape'
ष	ṣha	as *sh* in 'show'
स	sa	as *s* in 'sin'

Aspirate

| ह | ha | as *h* in 'hut' |

Visarga

| : | ḥ | it is a strong aspirate; also lengthens the preceding vowel and occurs only at the end of a word. It is pronounced as a final *h* sound |

Anusvara Nasalized

ं		m/n	nasalizes and lengthens the preceding vowel and is pronounced as *n* in the words 'and' or 'anthem'
ँ		~	as *n* in 'gung-ho'

Avagraha

ऽ		'	This is a silent character indicating अ. It is written but not pronounced; used in specific combination (sandhi) rules

Others

क्ष	kṣha	as *ksh* in 'freakshow'
ज्ञ	jña	as *gy* in 'bigyoung'
ड़	ṛa	There is no sign in English to represent the sound ड़. It has been written as *ṛa*, but the tip of the tongue quickly flaps down
ढ़	ṛha	There is no sign in English to represent the sound ढ़. It has been written as *ṛha*, but the tip of the tongue quickly flaps down
श्र	śhra	as *śhra* in 'śhravan'
त्र	tra	as *tra* in 'mantra'
ज़	z	as *z* in the word 'zaroor'

Let's Connect

If you enjoyed reading this book and would like to connect with Swami Mukundananda, you can do so through any of the following channels:

Websites: *www.jkyog.org*, *www.jkyog.in*, *www.swamimukundananda.org*

YouTube channels: 'Swami Mukundananda' and 'Swami Mukundananda Hindi'

Facebook: 'Swami Mukundananda' and 'Swami Mukundananda Hindi'

Instagram: 'Swami Mukundananda' and 'Swami Mukundananda Hindi'

Pinterest: Swami Mukundananda – JKYog

Telegram: Swami Mukundananda

Twitter: Swami Mukundananda (@Sw_Mukundananda)

LinkedIn: Swami Mukundananda

Audio Podcasts: Apple, SoundCloud, Spotify

JKYog Radio: TuneIn app for iOS and Android

JKYog App: Available for iOS and Android

WhatsApp Daily Inspirations: We have two broadcast lists. You are welcome to join either or both.

    India: +91 84489 41008
    USA: +1 346-239-9675

Online Classes:

    JKYog India: *www.jkyog.in/online-sessions/*
    JKYog US: *www.jkyog.org/online-classes*

Email: deskofswamiji@swamimukundananda.org

To bring Swami Mukundananda's teachings to your organization—as Amazon, Google, Intel, Microsoft, Oracle, Verizon, United Nations, Stanford University, Yale University, IITs and IIMs have done—look us up at sm-leadership.org.